"This is a thoroughly helpf[...] a lot of time listening to th[...] questions they actually ask (which are not always the questions we pastors want them to ask!). Matt Fuller engages the reader with a light touch and earthy pastoral realism, behind which lie a clear theological mind and careful study."

Christopher Ash, *Writer-in-Residence at Tyndale House and Ministry Trainer at St. Andrew the Great, Cambridge and author of "Zeal Without Burnout"*

"Christians struggle if we fail to believe in both the wonderful status given us forever when we are born again *and* the fact that the Lord responds to how we then live. Matt Fuller's book is an accessible, down-to-earth, sustained reflection on how we can keep these important truths together."

Garry Williams, *Director of The John Owen Centre, London Theological Seminary*

"Matt Fuller has done a superb job in taking us to the point where our unconditional, unearned and secure status in Christ meets our dynamic, progressive transformation in Christ-likeness. This book is clearly written, drenched in pastoral concern, answering real questions and coloured with helpful illustrations. It's the book I wanted to write— and it's a book I loved reading."

Ray Galea, *Lead Pastor, St Alban's MBM, Australia*

"How can we be sure that our status before God is unchanging (we are justified) when our personal walk with the Lord is so erratic (we still sin)? If Christ has paid the penalty for all our sin, then why do we need to confess it? With penetrating insight and a pastor's heart, Matt mines the treasure of the precious doctrine of justification by faith alone and encourages us to keep working out our salvation, secure in the knowledge that we are God's children if we trust him to the end."

Carrie Sandom, *Associate Minister for Women at St John's, Tunbridge Wells and Director of Women's Ministry at the Proclamation Trust, London*

"Reading *Perfect Sinners* brought so much joy to my soul. It's not only biblically rich and beautifully written with quite brilliant stories and illustrations. It addresses supremely important questions that members of our congregations often ask about salvation in Christ: questions about God's love and our failure, about justification and transformation, about guilt and assurance, about falling away and discipline. This is not just a heart-warming read—Matt has given us a really important book which clarifies the nature of saving faith in simple language for a new generation. I absolutely love it!"

Richard Coekin, *Senior Pastor of Dundonald Church and Director of Co-Mission in London*

"Matt Fuller explains and applies the beautiful gem of justification by faith in ways that will help you love Jesus more. Many of the issues we struggle with—doubt, assurance, half-heartedness, joylessness, guilt, disobedience—are shown to be issues related to justification and are addressed in helpful, practical, clear ways. I wholeheartedly recommend this excellent work."

Tim Rudge, *Field Director, UCCF*

"Guilt and grace, faith and works, justification and sanctification, warnings and assurance... How do these things fit together? 500 years after the start of the Reformation, many remain confused about such matters. Clear, insightful, engaging, pastoral and, most importantly, biblical—*Perfect Sinners* is a timely antidote for such confusion."

Rob Smith, *Lecturer in Theology and Ethics, Sydney Missionary & Bible College*

"Here's a book that will benefit Christians, whatever our stage of following Christ. No quick fixes. Instead, a thoroughgoing biblical call to persevering faith and trust in Christ, and a developing grasp of what it means to be accepted in the Beloved."

Trevor Archer, *London Director, FIEC*

Matt Fuller

PERFECT

SINNERS

See yourself as God sees you

Dedicated to the memory of John Fuller.
I'm thankful for the constancy and sacrifice
of your fatherhood.
I never doubted your love for me.
I'm thrilled to have made you proud.

Perfect Sinners *See yourself as God sees you*
© Matt Fuller/The Good Book Company, 2017.
Reprinted 2017.

Published by
The Good Book Company
Tel (UK): 0333 123 0880
International: +44 (0) 208 942 0880
Email: info@thegoodbook.co.uk

Websites:
North America: www.thegoodbook.com
UK: www.thegoodbook.co.uk
Australia: www.thegoodbook.com.au
New Zealand: www.thegoodbook.co.nz

Cover design by Ben Woodcraft

ISBN: 9781784981389 | Printed in the UK

Contents

What does God think of me?

"What does he think of me?"

This can be a crucial question.

It's an anxious question when we've been interviewed for a job: "Did the interviewers like me? Err... I think so, but they did frown when I said I hated hard work." The interviewers' verdict can make or break us.

It's a nervous question when we've performed a piece of music for an exam, or publicly for a crowd, and we wonder, "Will I pass?" or, "What did they think of me?"

It's a burning question when there's someone we like romantically: "I've dropped heavy hints. I kept gazing awkwardly at them. So, what do they think of me?"

In all these cases, someone else's opinion matters intensely. It can feel like the only thing that matters.

But nothing affects us in the same way as: "What does God think of me?" His opinion utterly transforms our lives *now* and determines our future in *eternity*.

Nothing matters more.

I recently sat with a man with only a few weeks to live. I asked if he expected to go to heaven when he died. It was a sobering conversation because, at the end of your life, only one thing matters: "What does God think of me?" His verdict determines our eternal destiny.

As well as our destiny, the knowledge of God's verdict *then* is meant to profoundly affect our lives *now*. More than anyone else's opinion, understanding God's approval can transform how we think, feel and act.

I remember my first job interview, at the age of 22 (I'm not counting a paper round). It was pretty intense but that night they rang and offered me the job and a salary. I accepted, put down the phone and giggled. No one had paid me proper money before! I could move city, rent a home, and buy dinner out—a whole new world opened up for me. The opinion of the interview panel had an obvious impact on my life.

A few years later I asked my girlfriend to marry me. After an unsettling period of delay, the answer was happily yes and I was dancing on clouds. The fact that someone was willing to commit to a lifetime of marriage to me was a source of wonder to myself (and many others).

These verdicts upon me affected me deeply and made significant changes to my life. Yet, God's opinion has an *incomparable* capacity to transform your life.

Of course God loves me, but... err...

As Christians, we sometimes get confused about how God thinks of us. So we ask ourselves, and each other:

Q: I'm a Christian; so God loves me in Jesus. Is there really nothing I can do to make him love me more or less?

Q: Does God love all Christians the same?

Q: Should I ever feel guilty? Is that appropriate?

Q: If I'm always forgiven, what's going on when I confess sin? Am I even more forgiven?

Q: Do some Christians get greater reward in heaven? How come? Where does grace fit in?

Q: If God will never let me go, why does the Bible warn against falling away? Am I in danger of turning away from God?

These questions are asked by Christians who know that God's verdict upon our lives is meant to bring enormous joy. But we're never entirely sure what his view of us is.

At the heart of these questions is a blurring of our "status before God" and our daily "walk with God". I've compared them in the table below. Everything on the status side became true when you became a Christian and will remain true into eternity. By contrast, our walk with God changes regularly; perhaps on a daily basis (or even hourly). Our godliness is not constant; nor is our experience of God.

Our status is deliberately in capitals because, in a healthy Christian, it's our status before God that gives us confidence that God loves us. When we allow our walk with God to shape how we imagine he views us, then we'll wobble and be anxious.

OUR STATUS BEFORE GOD	Our walk with God
UNCHANGING	Fluctuating
UNCONDITIONAL	Conditional
JUSTIFIED	Progressively sanctified
FATHER'S LOVE FOR US	Father's pleasure with us or displeasure
FORGIVEN	Fluctuating guilt/forgiveness
WE ARE DECLARED HOLY	We are growing in holiness

In this book we'll pull apart our "status" before God and our "walk" with him. Both come from being "in Christ". We're united to Jesus as a branch is to a tree. All spiritual life flows from him to us. Yet the distinction between "status" and "walk" is key.

500 years ago, Martin Luther started the Reformation with the discovery that he was *simul justus et peccator*. I only know this one Latin phrase, but it's a good one. It means we're simultaneously justified before the Lord and yet still a sinner. This is true of every Christian. We are:

Perfect: our status before the Lord never changes. We are always righteous before him and so he loves us deeply.

Sinners: our walk before the Lord is highly variable, which is why we sometimes feel guilty and wonder what God thinks of us.

It's because we're both *perfect* and *sinful* that the godly person is genuinely excited to know God as Father and yet bewildered by the times when they don't care about him. They are thrilled by the promises in the gospel and yet despair over how often they doubt them. Sadly, that's normal Christian living. We should long to change but not despair that change takes time.

Holding both together

Even when we mentally get our heads around being both perfect and sinners, living it out is hard. Most Christians (and churches) lean in one direction more than the other. Consider two absurdly named people: "Status Steve" and "Walking Wendy".

"Status Steve" is rock solid on the truth that God has accepted him through Jesus. He's an upbeat chap who sings loads of Christian songs and enjoys his church, where he is affirmed. This is great! The downside is that he doesn't really consider how to love and serve others or how God wants him to change. Steve is confident that God loves him whatever he does and so he mostly does whatever he wants, even when the Bible tells him not to. Because, hey, God always loves him, so what does it matter if he sleeps with his girlfriend and gets drunk most weekends?!

By contrast, "Walking Wendy" is obsessed by how well she's living the Christian life. She assesses her obedience daily. She's always looking to repent of anything that doesn't please the Lord. She daily confesses all she's done wrong and seeks to express her love for God by obeying him. This is great! The downside is that she's anxious and introspective. She seems happier reciting a confession than singing a hymn of praise.

Both of these are caricatures, but they help us to have some idea of which way we lean. Of course, it's possible to flit between being a "Steve" and a "Wendy": sometimes feeling secure in our status before God, but other times obsessing about our walk with him. Yet the Christian life is healthiest when both are combined so that we're aware both of being perfect in status and also a sinner in our Christian walk. Not aware of this just formally as doctrines we believe, but practically as truths that affect how we live. It's surprisingly hard to get right.

We're going to spend the first three chapters focusing upon our status before God. We need to have that clearly and joyfully in place before we get into the often more confusing areas about how we live this truth out.

Which means we need to start in the courtroom...

1. How can God love me when he hates sin?

Only once have I spent time in court. To be clear, it wasn't for my own crime—I was on jury service.

We were a pretty odd bunch. One woman was so terrified she couldn't swear her oath. Another juror was clearly distracted and it emerged she was listening to an iPod under her headscarf. I was "Mr Keen", diligently making notes, so I was pathetically pleased with myself when elected jury foreman. That was, until the moment I had to deliver the verdict.

We had deliberated over the evidence and made our decision. The judge asked me to stand and deliver a verdict: "Do you find the defendant guilty or not guilty?" I looked at the 30-year-old man in the dock. I don't suppose I'll say another single word with the same impact in the whole of my life.

"Guilty."

The defendant was taken away for a lengthy spell in prison.

The Bible is clear that one day all of us will appear in God's courtroom:

> Now we know that whatever the law says, it says to
> those who are under the law, so that every mouth may
> be silenced and the whole world held accountable to
> God. Therefore no one will be declared righteous in
> God's sight by the works of the law; rather, through the
> law we become conscious of our sin. (Romans 3 v 19-20)

We're all in trouble before God's law. That means we're in trouble with him. Of course, the Bible talks about our relationship with God in many ways. But underpinning many other ways of explaining how God thinks of us, the Bible clearly uses the language of the courtroom. We are facing God's judgment.

We need to get this clear in order to rightly enjoy everything the Bible tells us about God's love for us. The moment you devalue the seriousness of God's justice, you undermine the wonder of his love in rescuing us.

A desperate need

The greatest need of every human is God. To stand before him we need "righteousness". Although this is a key Bible word, it's not much used in everyday English. All of us dislike someone who is "self-righteous". Those of a certain vintage may enjoy the songs of pop duo the "Righteous Brothers". Alternatively, I hear the word used in the slang of local kids: "Ah, that curry was righteous". (I think they mean it was good.)

So, what does the Bible mean?

In simple terms, it means a right standing before God. He is perfectly righteous and so, if we're to be with him, we need to have that righteousness too.

The same little word gets translated different ways in English. At a basic level, you might say:

Righteous = justified = not guilty

Paul contrasts being righteous/justified with being condemned (Romans 5 v 16)—so to be righteous is the opposite of being guilty. But that doesn't fully capture it.

Think of it like this. When I was a juror, we found a 30-year-old man guilty, so he was condemned to eight years in prison. He had naturally hoped to be found "not guilty". In that case, he would have been free to go. Free to go back to the life he had before.

But imagine if the judge stepped in and said, "You're not simply 'not guilty'; you're *justified* before me. You're not merely 'free to go' but you're 'free to come'. You're free to come to my house and stay. Plus, because I'm a wealthy judge, you're free to stay in any of my houses around the world. You're free to dine at my expense at any restaurant you desire. What's more, you're free to call me any time you're in trouble. You're free to make any request of me at all. You are righteous before me. Not merely free to go, but free to come and enjoy all the benefits of knowing me."

The difference is enormous!

To be righteous before God is to be in right standing before him. We enjoy complete access and all the benefits of knowing him. We're free to come.

The big problem for you and me is... that we *are* guilty, and, by nature, unable to come to God. So, how can God, the perfect and righteous judge, forgive us without compromising justice? How can he call us righteous when we're guilty?

In a human court, we'd be outraged if a jury found a man guilty of rape but then the judge said, "I'm in a forgiving mood. So let's just call you innocent—and you're free to come and have a cup of tea with me." There would be howls of protest at such a miscarriage of justice. Similarly, God cannot just say, "I'm going to forgive guilty sinners. Let's pretend nothing ever went wrong." It would destroy his just character.

So we have this central question: How can God display justice and mercy at the same time? Or to re-phrase it in personal terms: *How can God love me when he hates sin?*

Let's answer this by looking at Romans 3, and then making three contrasting statements.

> But now apart from the law the righteousness of God has been made known, to which the Law and the Prophets testify. This righteousness is given through faith in Jesus Christ to all who believe. There is no difference between Jew and Gentile, for all have sinned and fall short of the glory of God, and all are justified freely by his grace through the redemption that came by Christ Jesus. God presented Christ as a sacrifice of atonement, through the shedding of his blood—to be received by faith. He did this to demonstrate his righteousness, because in his forbearance he had left the sins committed beforehand unpunished—he did it to demonstrate his righteousness at the present time, so as to be just and the one who justifies those who have faith in Jesus. (Romans 3 v 21-26)

1. God hates sinners and he loves sinners

Before we look at how God combines justice and mercy, we'll pause to consider how he views us before we become Christians. Romans 3 v 23 tells us that, "All have sinned and fall short of the glory of God". So, how did God view us when we sinned?

The Bible insists that before anyone becomes a Christian, God both loved us and he hated us. That's strong language, I know. We want to resist it, because we like to think we're naturally loveable. Yet, from God's perspective, we're not. Consider these verses (bold text mine):

> The arrogant cannot stand in your presence. You hate all who do wrong; you destroy those who tell lies. The bloodthirsty and deceitful **you, LORD, detest**. (Psalm 5 v 5-6)

> The LORD examines the righteous, but the wicked, those who love violence, **he hates with a passion**. (Psalm 11 v 5)

> Whoever believes in the Son has eternal life, but whoever rejects the Son will not see life, for **God's wrath remains on them**. (John 3 v 36)

Those are strong words: The Lord detests and hates sinners. His wrath or anger remains on them. There are two common objections to this:

First, people often say, "God hates the sin but loves the sinner". But these verses show that's not true when someone isn't a Christian. We cannot separate our actions from who we are. We're not good people who occasionally sin. We are "sinners".

We would laugh at a compulsive liar who said, "I always tell the truth, but sometimes lies pop out from me." We'd reply, "No, take ownership of your lies. They're not separate from you. They're not like little frogs jumping out of your pocket. They belong to you. You are a liar."

Or we'd be bewildered by the constantly angry person who said, "I'm a calm person, but sometimes anger bubbles up inside of me". We'd respond, "No, take ownership of your anger".

In the same way, all of our sin belongs to us. It is fundamentally a part of us—a reflection of who we are. Jesus describes our words as coming from us. Our sinful words are not distinct from us; they are a part of us:

> A good man brings good things out of the good stored
> up in his heart, and an evil man brings evil things out
> of the evil stored up in his heart. For the mouth speaks
> what the heart is full of. (Luke 6 v 45)

We are born as sinners—and God hates sinners. It's part of our identity.

The second common objection is to the idea of God being angry or wrathful: "I like the idea of God as love. But I don't like the idea of him being wrathful."

Yet God's wrath is his personal reaction to sin. One drawback with focusing on the law-court imagery is that in a court the judge is meant to be neutral and not personally involved. We would never allow someone to sit as a judge in a murder trial if the victim had been his daughter. He'd be far too close to the case.

Yet God *is* personally involved. Our sin is a personal assault upon the Lord—as we reject his laws and trust ourselves instead. And yet he is a perfect judge, never mastered by emotions. He is *both* personally affronted by our sin *and* perfectly just in his sentencing. No human could manage both. In a helpful phrase of the late preacher John Stott, God's wrath is "his steady, unrelenting, unremitting, uncompromising, *personal* antagonism to evil in all its forms and manifestations" (*The Cross of Christ*).

So, before I became a Christian in April 1993, God hated me because I was a guilty rebel. I was under his anger or wrath... and yet... at the same time... he loved me.

It's easy to sing of God's amazing love for us. Yet it's only when we understand his hatred of us as sinners that we can see the depths of quite how wonderful and unlikely his love is. The perfect, holy God sees all that we are as sinners. Nothing is hidden from him. The full filth of our lives and the complete extent of our rejection of him are transparent. And still he loves us.

Deep down we all want to believe there's something inherently appealing in us. We assume that God is drawn to us *a little bit* by our innate qualities. But he did not look down upon us from heaven and think, "They're wicked—and yet so lovely that I'm drawn to love them". No, we are worthless (see Romans 3 v 10-20). *God loves us purely because he is loving.*

Before I was a Christian, God loved me and he hated me. The moment I became a Christian and trusted Jesus' work for me, all God's hatred and wrath was removed, and all that remains for me is his love. The same is true for every Christian.

How does that work?

2. God the Father punishes his Son and justifies sinners

Here is how God can punish sin and yet declare us in right standing (righteous) before him. The familiar truth at the heart of the Christian message is the great exchange upon the cross.

There are moments in life when I flippantly think I'd like to exchange lives with someone else. I was recently stuck in traffic for hours going nowhere when a friend sent a picture of him and his family playing on a beautiful beach. At that moment, I'd have gladly swapped my situation for his.

At one level, the exchange upon the cross is that simple.

1. Christ took upon himself our sin and so endured God's wrath.
2. We receive Christ's righteousness upon us and so enjoy God's blessing.

Romans 3 v 25 is central in revealing how God can be just as he does this:

God presented Christ as a sacrifice of atonement, through the shedding of his blood—to be received by

> faith. He did this to demonstrate his righteousness,
> because in his forbearance he had left the sins
> committed beforehand unpunished. (Romans 3 v 25)

We've said that, in a human court, a judge can't just let a criminal off when he's guilty. The same is true for the God of perfect justice. God *will punish* sin. The cross is the place where he has done that, while also showing mercy. No single illustration captures the wonder of this completely. We'll need many throughout this book to try and get a balanced picture. But for a start, think of it this way:

In the 19th century, a man was conscripted to serve overseas in the army. He had just married, so a friend kindly stepped in as a substitute. The friend served nobly for several years until tragically dying in battle. Some time later the original man was conscripted for a second time but refused to serve. He appeared in court and pleaded that his friend had already gone in his place, served in the war, and indeed had been killed in his place. He pleaded that his friend served and died *for him and as him.* Therefore justice had been done and it would be unjust to make him serve and die a second time. As the story goes, the judge agreed and the man was free to go. His role had been taken and paid for.

Similarly, Jesus has exchanged places with the Christian. Legally, God has punished my sin "in Christ" and he will not punish me twice.

Let's push that further. The Bible insists that when the Christian's sin is punished "in Christ" we are also crucified with him (Galatians 2 v 20). Not physically, but spiritually in our union with him. Think of it this way:

A few years ago a plane took off near St Louis, Missouri, but hit a power cable causing an engine to burst into flames. There were six passengers on board for a skydiving lesson, but the plane was never going to climb high enough for a safe jump. The quick-thinking dive instructor was a man named Robert Cook. He grabbed hold of one of the divers called Kim Dear. He strapped himself to her and, as the plane was about to crash, made sure he was beneath her to take the impact of the ground. His body was crushed but she survived. Kim Dear was united to her saviour, who died so that she might live. Again, no illustration is perfect, but we must remember that it is by being united to Jesus that we obtain the benefits of his work.

When we're united to Christ, he takes our punishment and we receive his righteousness.

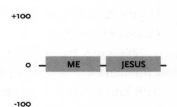

It's **not** that, before we trust in Jesus, we have a tragic moral score of -100...

Jesus has great moral score of +100...

...and when he died for us, he cancelled out our negative, and so we're now neutral.

NO!

Rather, Jesus took our -100, and we receive his +100.

Wonderfully, this is a status that does not vary and cannot be lost.

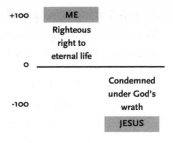

Back in the Garden of Eden, there was a time when Adam had done nothing wrong. He had a perfect relationship with God. Yet it was always possible for him to muck up morally. He was always on probation.

Some people will know that experience. Often, when you start a job, you're put on a three-month probation period. You've done nothing wrong but you have no security either. It can be an anxious time, as you know that your performance is being watched and assessed. It's a relief when you pass your period of probation and become a permanent employee with greater rights.

For you and me, we are **not** on probation as Adam was. When you become a Christian and join "God PLC", you're given the lifetime service record of Jesus Christ. You can never be sacked. You have 10,000 years of brilliant service on your file. You have all the pay and pension rights of a star employee. It's impossible for the boss to view you with anything but love and delight.

Or, to return to a legal picture, we *don't* live life on trial, uncertain of what God's verdict will be in the future. The verdict is in already—and it's that we're justified, righteous and free to come.

When we trust in Jesus' work on the cross, we are not merely pardoned; we are positively *righteous*. We are perfect in God's sight.

It's a legal verdict upon us. It's a permanent change of status. It's 100% certainty that God accepts us.

3. God displays justice and shows mercy

The great exchange upon the cross is how God combines justice and mercy. As Paul writes:

> He did this to demonstrate his righteousness, because in his forbearance he had left the sins committed beforehand unpunished—he did it to demonstrate his righteousness at the present time, so as to be just and the one who justifies those who have faith in Jesus.
> (Romans 3 v 25-26)

The sins of Old Testament believers such as Abraham, Moses and David were left unpunished in history. Jesus pays for all of them on the cross too.

Here is the union of infinite love with inflexible justice. The wonder of this is that when we appear before God the Father as judge, we're not going to be pleading for mercy. John describes Jesus as our advocate before the Father (1 John 2 v 1). If you ever needed a lawyer, God himself, Christ the Son, is the best possible one. The picture here is that when we stand in God's courtroom at the end of history, Jesus is our lawyer, God the Father is judge, and there's no doubt about the verdict.

This is a scene they planned together before the creation of the world! When we stand in God's courtroom, it is not that Jesus' great love is pleading against the Father's stern justice. Jesus is not twisting the arm of an unwilling Father. Instead, Jesus pleads for justice: *This man or woman is indeed guilty, but I have paid in full for their crimes and they are righteous.* The Father replies, *Yes, this is how I lovingly bestow mercy.*

How can God love you when he hates your sin? He can do so because on the cross he has justly punished your sin and granted you Jesus' righteousness. Your status has changed.

That may not sound exciting. It may not immediately affect the way we feel and act. But it should and it will because justification isn't *merely* the transfer of a quality from Jesus to us; it's intimacy with him as we're united by faith.

Imagine a millionaire who catches a scamp breaking into his house. He kindly decides that, rather than have him arrested, he will adopt him as his own child. Legally the boy becomes his son. Now, there is no biological or moral change within the boy. His genetic make-up isn't affected, but his status certainly is. Although it's a legal change, it affects *everything* about the boy's status and his happiness and his future. It's a truth that *will* shape his character over time.

We're not just pardoned; we're loved. We're not just innocent but adopted. We're not just liberated but awarded the right to eternal life.

So, don't live life as though on trial before God, uncertain of his verdict. The verdict is in and God says, *You're righteous. A perfect sinner. Come near and enjoy me.*

2. How strong does my faith need to be?

Your faith does not justify you.

That's perhaps a surprising statement, so let me explain.

My wife, Ceri, suffers with vertigo. I've tried to help her overcome it. I even persuaded her to go on the *London Eye* Ferris wheel a couple of years ago—but she says it's not a fun experience when you sit in the middle of the carriage, gripping the seat, with your eyes shut, for 40 minutes.

If we go up a turret in an old castle and look out from the top, she'll freak out and scream, "Hold on to the children". Logically it's quite hard for a toddler to leap over a one-metre-high wall, but that's the thing about irrational fears... they're irrational. As Ceri describes it, her legs turn completely to jelly on top of a castle turret and she feels as if she's going to fall.

Yet she's made progress. She can now tell herself, "This castle has stood here for hundreds of years. My legs may fail, but I really can trust the walls. As long as they don't collapse, no one is going to die." Eventually that truth does break through the fear. Though her legs feel weak, she stops freaking out and occasionally even enjoys the view. The truth she needs to know is that her safety doesn't depend on her legs, but upon the castle's solid walls.

Look at Jesus, not at yourself

It's easy to live the Christian life looking at our legs rather than at the solid ground. So we worry about the strength of our faith, rather than looking at the object of our faith: Jesus. Partly that's a problem with Christian shorthand. We often use the phrase: "We're justified by faith". Happily that *does not* mean that we're justified by the quality of our faith. It *does* mean that we're justified by faith **in Jesus**.

It would be a disaster if it was the quality of our faith that put us in right standing with God. Sometimes our faith feels strong; sometimes it feels weak. Sometimes we trust the Lord in our actions; sometimes we don't. Our faith is highly variable. So it's a relief that our salvation doesn't rest upon the quality of our faith, but upon Jesus! *Our faith may go to jelly, but he is the solid ground upon which we stand.*

We're continuing to think about our **status** before the Lord. In chapter 1 we saw that we have a legal verdict of being in right standing with him. That cannot vary, fluctuate or change. The great exchange upon the cross means that Jesus has taken our punishment and we have received his righteousness. It's not merely that our debt is paid, but we're made billionaires. It's not merely that we're set free from prison, but we're set upon a throne. It's not merely that God removes my moral deformity; he views me as morally beautiful.

But we need to be clear upon the answers to these questions:

Q: What do we contribute to our righteous status?
A: Nothing.

Q: So, what does our faith contribute?

A: Faith *contributes* nothing. It merely connects us to Jesus.

Faith is work-less: it contributes nothing. Faith is worthless, unless it is faith in Christ.

I used to work with a woman who hated flying. Before any flight she'd take several tablets of valium to calm her nerves. On take off, she'd close her eyes and grip my hand until I wanted to scream with pain. By contrast, I've never been a nervous flyer. Yet at the end of the flight, both of us arrived at the same destination. For her it had been stressful; for me (apart from a sore hand) it was very relaxing. I was confident in my faith in the plane. She was not. But we both got there. Our faith is somewhat like our confidence in flying. Jesus takes us to heaven whether our faith is strong or anxious.

I know too many Christians who spend a lot of time worrying about their faith. It is **not** the strength of your faith that brings you righteousness. It is the strength of your Saviour.

Why we don't like this much

There's something in us that deeply battles against this truth. Faith is massively important in the writings of the apostle Paul. He uses the word 142 times, and the verb "to believe" 54 times. Often it's used to contrast two ways to be justified (given a right standing before God). Paul stresses that this is by faith and not by works.

> [21] But now apart from the law the righteousness of God has been made known, to which the Law and the Prophets testify. [22] This righteousness is given through faith in Jesus Christ to all who believe. There is no difference between Jew and Gentile, [23] for all have sinned and fall short of the glory of God, [24] and all are justified

freely by his grace through the redemption that came by
Christ Jesus. (Romans 3 v 21-24)

Paul is clear in verses 21-22 that our right standing before God
does not come from what we do (obedience to the law) but through
faith in Jesus Christ. But even if we've been a Christian for decades,
there's something in us that kicks back against that truth.

A friend went to theological college in the US. In her
first year, she took a course on New Testament theology and
justification by faith. At the end of the semester, the lecturer set
a fair but tough exam. On results day, everyone's exam marks
were posted publicly on a wall. It was a brutal way to find out
that... everyone had failed. Every student without exception!

Before long there were 100 students outside the teacher's office.
Some were in tears; others were angry, saying, "It was too tough".

Eventually the lecturer appeared and calmly asked, "Was
there anything in this exam that was not on the syllabus?"
Silence. He followed up: "If you want to see model answers that
would have secured a grade A, I've written them and stapled
them to the back of your exam scripts." He then handed back all
their papers with a percentage and grade on the front of each.

The students read them out loud to one another: "20%, grade
A", "32%, grade A", "15%, grade A". They began to mumble in
bewilderment: "What's going on? We've all failed and yet you've
given us an A grade." The teacher waited some time before
saying, "During the last few months, I've taught you theology.
You've given your mental assent but I never felt you celebrated
this truth or that it brought you joy. So in this exam I decided to
teach you, once again, the most important lesson in the whole
of life. None of you could pass the exam on your own merits.
You needed me to give you my wisdom. So you were awarded
a grade you don't deserve. So, here's what I want you to truly
know and feel: *You cannot be saved by your own works or efforts.*

You need Jesus to give you his righteousness."

My friend tells me this was greeted with a variety of responses. Some laughed. Some sighed. Apparently one person was still a bit peeved, saying, "It's not fair that I scored 38% and got the same grade as someone on 15%. I don't want the same grade as them." It had to be pointed out that he'd *really failed* to understand the teacher's point. A fail is a fail, no matter how far short you are. All of them needed the gift.

Of course, there's a profound irony in a group of people taking a course in New Testament theology but failing to understand the basics of being saved by faith and not by works. Yet it just shows how hard we find it to truly believe this.

There's a contrast between faith and works

Certainly, some in Rome struggled to believe that it was not their own works that gave them a right standing with God. It seems there were some Jewish converts in the church who were asking about Abraham. Surely, they argue, Abraham was put right with God by his actions or works? Yet Paul insists not.

> [1] What then shall we say that Abraham, our forefather according to the flesh, discovered in this matter? [2] If, in fact, Abraham was justified by works, he had something to boast about—but not before God. [3] What does Scripture say? "Abraham believed God, and it was credited to him as righteousness."[4] Now to the one who works, wages are not credited as a gift but as an obligation. [5] However, to the one who does not work but trusts God who justifies the ungodly, their faith is credited as righteousness. (Romans 4 v 1-5)

The key argument comes in verse 3, where Paul quotes from Genesis 15. God promised Abraham that his offspring would be as many as the stars of the sky. What did Abraham do? He "**believed** God and it was **credited** to him as righteousness". Paul is saying that Abraham believed God's promise of many offspring, and so righteousness (a right standing before God) was placed in his spiritual bank account. Paul thinks that this *must* rule out any boasting. In verse 4, he gives an illustration to make his point. It's easy for us to understand:

Joe is an ordinary car salesman. On the 25th day of each month, his pay of £1600 arrives in his bank account, and he's given a pay slip showing how he's earned his salary.

That's not generosity. Joe's work has earned that money.

However, what if one of Joe's colleagues, called Kate, has a stellar year and sells a crazy number of cars? She single-handedly makes five million pounds for the car manufacturer and so receives a bonus of one million pounds. But as well as Kate being good at her job, she is kind. She splits her bonus with Joe so that he gets a half-million-pound bonus he hasn't earned.

Joe hasn't worked for that money. It's a generous gift.

So, Paul concludes, Abraham had not worked to earn his righteousness—he was credited it as a gift. *The faith that saves trusts in God's promises.* For Abraham, that was the promise of offspring. For you and me, it's the promise that God justifies the ungodly (v 5). Who is it that is justified (in right standing with God)? It's not the one who trusts his own behaviour, but the one who trusts in God to justify us.

Or as the students learned: *Don't trust in your exam score. Trust in the teacher's gift.*

The faith that saves trusts in God's promises
Let's dwell upon this phrase. It's so important to understand. Here are two similar-sounding definitions. One is the correct definition of **justified**; the other is not.

1. God made me righteous by imparting grace into my heart so that I can do good works that put me in right standing before God.
2. God declared me righteous by counting Christ's good works to my account and my sins to his so that I'm in right standing with God.

Are you clear which is which? We're into the important difference between our *status* before God and our *walk* with God. The first statement states that righteousness is a process that takes place inside of us. The second statement (the correct one!) says that righteousness is a legal status conferred outside of us.

It's a bit like, in statement one, Jesus comes along and gives you a load of ingredients and tells you to bake a cake. If the cake is good enough, God will accept you. In the second statement, Jesus comes along and gives you a cake. A perfect finished cake. Your contribution is... nothing. Now, I'm a rubbish cook and know I can never bake a decent cake. I need someone to give me theirs. Morally, all of us are sinners incapable of creating a righteous life. We need Jesus to give us his.

So, here's a good question to see if you really understand this: *How confident are you that God will accept you into heaven?* I've asked that of all sorts of people. Often the answer is, "I'm not sure... It varies from day to day... I used to hope so, but now I'm not too sure." If we understand what Paul is saying, our response should be, "I trust that Jesus has taken my sin and given me his righteousness, and so I'm 100% certain of God's acceptance, both now and on the day when I stand before him".

We're justified by faith in Jesus (not by faith)

Rather than using the shorthand expression, "We're justified by faith", it might be healthier to say, "Jesus justifies us by faith in him". It's a little clumsier but more accurate. It stops us looking at our own wobbly faith and helps us to look at him.

Martin Luther suggested that "faith clasps Christ as a ring clasps its jewel". It's a helpful picture. No one looks at a ring and comments upon the clasp. It's the jewel that sparkles; it's the jewel that's special; and it's the jewel that costs the money! The jewel is valuable and the clasp holds onto it. Yet, there's a greater degree of intimacy than that. Elsewhere the Bible compares this union of Christ with the believer to a vine and branches; to a head and body; to a husband and wife. Righteousness is not a substance thrown across the courtroom like a coat. It is intimacy with a person: Jesus. The union of marriage helps us understand this.

When I married my wife, I was united to her and gained access to all that belonged to her, including her family. I now have highly amusing in-laws. They own a nice house near the coast where I can now go and visit them. I can enjoy their company and their generous hospitality of food and wine. I can enjoy the benefits of walking the dramatic coastline and swimming in the sea.

The only reason I have access to them and their generosity is because I'm united to Ceri. These blessings are not mine by right, but only because I'm married to her. There have possibly been occasions when they are pleased to have me as a son-in-law. There have undoubtedly been occasions when they've thought that I'm a hopeless husband and a hopeless father. But I've never lost access to them or their generosity, because it doesn't depend upon me, but on the fact that I'm united to their daughter.

It's not the quality of your faith that makes you acceptable to God. It is Jesus who makes you acceptable, and Christians are united to him.

It's never the case that God looks down from heaven and thinks, *Wow, look at how strong her faith is; I'll reward her for that. I love her much more than that person with their puny faith.*

There are no degrees of righteousness. It's binary. You're justified (in right standing with God) or you're not. You're -100 or +100—there's nothing in between.

So don't ponder the quality of your faith. Look at Christ.

Don't look within, but look up and see Christ, your righteousness, sitting at God's right hand.

You are *not* justified by your faith, but by faith that unites you to Jesus, who justifies you.

So, boasting is excluded (and so is despair)

> Where, then, is boasting? It is excluded. Because of what law? The law that requires works? No, because of the "law" that requires faith. For we maintain that a person is justified by faith apart from the works of the law.
> (Romans 3 v 27-28)

Paul is clear. Knowing that right standing comes through faith in Jesus, rather than our own efforts, excludes all boasting. Not only boasting that we can save ourselves but also boasting that we're better than others. As the students in the US seminary found out, a fail is a fail, be it at 30% or 15%. There's just no room for boasting.

Yet, we Christians can tend to look down upon those who struggle with sin in different ways and, in so doing, puff ourselves up a little.

We had a girl at church who I'll call Amber. She was sleeping with her boyfriend despite knowing that was wrong. She was confronted by another girl at church (we'll call her Bea). Bea didn't approach Amber with gentleness or an obvious loving concern. She confronted her in a scandalised tone: "I cannot believe what you're doing. You know that's wrong; you're ignoring the Bible; you're discouraging others. You're a disgrace."

Amber turned back and declared, "God hates the proud. Pride is far worse than sexual sin. I shall stop sleeping with my boyfriend when you stop being proud. But I can't see that happening in a hurry. Take your own plank out of your eye before you speak to me!"

To be clear, this isn't a good model of pastoral counselling! Both girls are really only scandalised by one type of sin. They look down on anyone who struggles in areas where they don't. It's not a rarity in churches that people look down on those who struggle with different sins. It's a form of boasting, and it has to go. When we truly see that all of us are shocking failures in God's sight, and that it's only when we're united to Jesus by faith that we can stand before the Lord, boasting is excluded.

Yet despair and worry can be excluded too. All of us fluctuate in our faith, and there are times when we doubt that God can accept us. There's a man at our church that I'll call Raymond, whose attendance is patchy. On past occasions he has stated, "I don't feel like I belong in church. I just can't forget what I've done in the past. I can't ignore how I've lived. I can't let it go."

I don't want to be trite, but we always come back to this fact: "Raymond, it's not about you. It's about Jesus. Don't look at your own life. Don't look at your own faith. Stop looking at yourself and look at Jesus."

Most of us need to hear that, time and again—when we're going well and when we're feeling wobbly. *Stop looking at yourself and look at Jesus.*

3. Does God only love me because he has to?

Ed grew up in a happy Christian home with great parents, and can't remember a time he didn't call himself a Christian. Yet, he struggles to enjoy the idea of God as Father. At root, he keeps coming back to this thought: "God the Father doesn't really love me. Jesus has brought me into his family, but the Father only accepts me because he has to. He sees me as a disruptive nuisance child or an unwanted step-child that he has to endure."

Ed isn't alone in this. Plenty of Christians think of God as a begrudging Father who is obliged to accept us. This often comes from *only* thinking about salvation in legal language. Yet the Bible insists that we're saved by being "in Christ". It is in union with him that we're born again, justified, adopted, sanctified, preserved and finally glorified. So we're not meant to come to God in the purely legal categories of the courtroom. We're also meant to come to him as our Father, who loves us deeply.

The Father has always loved us

Ed needs to understand that, while the work of Jesus is all-important for our salvation, it does not make the Father love us. The work of Jesus *flows out* of the Father's love (although it's only through Christ that we receive it). Consider these famous verses:

> For God so loved the world that he gave his one and only Son, that whoever believes in him shall not perish but have eternal life. (John 3 v 16)

> [8] Whoever does not love does not know God, because God is love. [9] This is how God showed his love among us: he sent his one and only Son into the world that we might live through him. (1 John 4 v 8-9)

These are, rightly, well-loved verses. We're told in 1 John 4 v 8 that God **is** love. This must be a reference to God the Father because he sends the Son in verse 9. So, God the Father **is love**. The New Testament stresses this elsewhere: Paul concludes 2 Corinthians with these famous words of blessing:

> May the grace of the Lord Jesus Christ, and the love of God, and the fellowship of the Holy Spirit be with you all. (2 Corinthians 13 v 14)

- What's highlighted about Jesus is his *grace*.
- What's highlighted about the Spirit is his *fellowship* with us.
- What's highlighted about the Father is his *love*.

When we approach God as Father, we're meant to think, "Love. The Father is Love." His love for me is eternal. It existed before the creation of the world. His love for me is without end and without beginning. It cannot grow or decline. It is a free love that I don't deserve. It is an unchangeable love that does not waver. It is, mysteriously, a specific love. He chose to love *me* as his child; that's not true of everyone.

The old Puritan writer John Owen (1616 – 1683) has some helpful pictures of the Father's love coming before all else, summarised here:

- The Father is the fountain of all love. He is the irresistible and unstoppable source from which love pours out. Jesus is the one who draws water from the fountain and brings it to us. There is no other way to know the Father's love but through the work of Jesus.

- Jesus is the treasure trove where the Father deposits all the riches of his grace, taken from the bottomless pit of his eternal love. Jesus is the one who gives us access to this treasury of grace.

These pictures helpfully remind us that all we have comes through our union with Christ. Yet also, the origin of all these blessings is the Father's love. He has always loved us; there is nothing begrudging about it.

The Father *really does* delight in us

Behind Ed's feeling that God loves him reluctantly lurks the recognition that he is, and always will be in this life, a sinner. That's why he describes himself as a "nuisance child" that the Father has to endure. "God the Father doesn't really love *me*," says Ed. "He loves Jesus—and therefore tolerates me."

Now, there's a hint of truth to this statement (we'll certainly always be sinners until heaven). But the Bible expresses it far more positively: *The Father loves his Son, Jesus. I'm united to Jesus and therefore the Father genuinely loves me*. It's *not* that the Father merely tolerates you—he loves you because of the work of Jesus.

As Paul puts it in Ephesians 5:

> Husbands, love your wives, just as Christ loved the
> church and gave himself up for her to make her holy,
> cleansing her by the washing with water through the
> word, and to present her to himself as a radiant church,
> without stain or wrinkle or any other blemish, but holy
> and blameless. (Ephesians 5 v 25-27)

The church has no natural beauty of her own, but Jesus makes
her beautiful. Yet plenty of Christians don't take delight in
Jesus making us beautiful. They grumble at being told there's
no inherent beauty to us. A friend of mine, the theologian
Garry Williams, helpfully points out how daft this is. Such
thinking is a bit like a bride on her wedding day getting upset.
She has spent all morning having her beauty enhanced by
a gorgeous dress, extravagant make-up and a sensational
hair stylist, but then is offended when people tell her how
lovely she looks. Rather than enjoying the compliments, she
complains, "What was wrong with me before?"

It *is* a humbling truth to know we're not naturally lovely in
God's sight. Yet, it's perverse to complain about that when he
has loved us and Jesus makes us beautiful. And we *really are*
now lovely in God's sight.

As a young Christian, I was taught this definition: "To
be justified = just-as-if-I'd lived like Jesus". This helpfully
emphasises our legal status of a right standing with God.
And yet... it falls a little short because we really are "in
Christ" and he is "in us". The union is so profound that it
goes beyond the illustration of marriage where, speaking
of material possessions, the husband and wife declare, "All
that I have I share with you". The Bible compares this union
between Christ and a believer to a vine and its branches, and

to a head and its body. The union of Christ with the believer is so strong that the Father really does delight in us as he delights in his Son.

Dwell upon that! God the Father has loved his Son with a perfect intensity throughout eternity. As a Christian you are united to Jesus and the Father loves you as he loves his own Son. Or to put it another way: *you are adopted as a child of God.*

The Son secures our *status* of adoption

> 4 But when the set time had fully come, God sent his Son, born of a woman, born under the law, 5 to redeem those under the law, that we might receive adoption to sonship. 6 Because you are his sons, God sent the Spirit of his Son into our hearts, the Spirit who calls out, "*Abba*, Father". 7 So you are no longer a slave, but God's child; and since you are his child, God has made you also an heir. (Galatians 4 v 4-7)

Here again, we see the Father's activity of sending both the Son and the Spirit. He sent the Son to secure our *status* of adoption, and he sends the Spirit to help us *experience* adoption.

Paul explains that the Father sent Jesus to redeem us from the curse of the law (Galatians 3 v 13). But this was *so that* "we might receive adoption to sonship" (Galatians 4 v 4). That's a legal term meaning that you have full legal standing as if you are a natural son. (In the culture of the day, only a son would inherit.)

Adoption in the Roman world was a little different from that in ours. It was unusual then to adopt a child. Normally, a childless man adopted a mature young man to continue the family name and receive the family's fortune. Only the very wealthy bothered with adoption to prevent their name and legacy dying out. So, if you were adopted, you'd go from being a poor nobody to a very wealthy somebody.

The process required seven witnesses, which made it very hard to undo. The adoptive father couldn't one day, in a moment of exasperation, say, "I'm fed up with you; I'm disinheriting you". It was a permanent legal change of status.

It's just the same for you and me. We are legally adopted children. Adoption flows inevitably out of being justified and in right standing with God. We are loved by, always accompanied by and given great honour by our heavenly Father.

But although we're adopted as children of God, sometimes we still *feel* like orphans. We need to grow in confidence of how wonderful our adoption is.

The Spirit helps us *experience* adoption

> Because you are his sons, God sent the Spirit of his Son
> into our hearts, the Spirit who calls out, "*Abba*, Father".
> (Galatians 4 v 6)

There's no delay between the moment of becoming a Christian and the moment the Father sends the Spirit of his Son into our hearts. It's instantaneous. No one becomes a Christian without the Spirit. The Christian has such a unity with Christ the Son that the Spirit of Christ has taken up residence in our hearts.

We may take this familiar truth for granted—but it's extraordinary.

We can be a little like a brother and sister who were clearing out their deceased parents' house in west London. An old jar had sat on a cupboard for the whole of their childhood, but they thought it might be worth a few pounds, so took it to a local auction house. It turned out to be an 18th-century Chinese *Qianlong* ceramic that sold for £51 million. When the hammer fell at auction, the brother had to be taken out for fresh air after nearly fainting.

For 40 years this family had no idea of the treasure within their house or how it could radically change their lives.

Christians can naively live that way too—going through life without enjoying the glorious riches of Christ's Spirit dwelling within them.

Paul tells us in Galatians 4 v 4-6 that, because of Christ's work done *outside of us* upon the cross, we have the status of adoption. That can never change. Yet, also because of that work of Christ, we have the Spirit *within us* affecting how we feel about being children of God. That experience will ebb and flow. Christ came to dwell in your heart by his Spirit at the moment you became a Christian—and yet the enjoyment of the love of Christ, and the knowledge of his presence, must be experienced in an ongoing fashion.

The Spirit grants an intimacy with God as Father. The Spirit causes us to cry out "*Abba*, Father", the same words of address that Jesus used in the Garden of Gethsemane (Mark 14 v 36). We can relate to God in the same way Jesus related to his Father because we have the Spirit of Jesus within us.

Many of us know it's possible to live the Christian life formally but without intimacy. A child may grow up in a very formal house with her parents. She knows she's their daughter, but it's a cold, loveless house. She's aware they've provided for her needs and committed to leave her an inheritance, but there's a cool distance between the girl and her parents. There's begrudging respect, but not love.

There's a world of difference between this and a house and family where there's obvious and demonstrable affection. Here, the child is greeted each day with enveloping hugs, a keen interest in conversation, and evident love. Even in his teen years, when he's embarrassed by his parents hugging him in public, the boy still quietly enjoys the fact that they so obviously care for him.

I don't want to drift into whimsy, but God is such a good Father that he's not content with informing us that we have the status of adopted children. He wants that status to affect us daily in our hearts. A deep understanding of our *status* must affect how we *walk* with God.

In his lovely book, *Adopted for life,* Russell Moore tells the moving story of how he and his wife adopted two toddlers from a Russian orphanage. After struggling through an enormous amount of red tape, they flew out to collect the boys—two little children who'd only ever lived in one room and had never been outside the orphanage. He describes their terror when he carried them outside. Neither had ever seen the sun nor felt the wind on their faces. The boys reached back with their hands to the only life they'd ever known. Naturally they were confused and scared.

It took these children a long time to settle into their new life in America but, in a telling description, Russell says that he and his wife knew the boys had acclimatised to their new home when they stopped hiding food in their high chairs. During their time in the orphanage, they'd learned that meals only came irregularly and so they hid food for later. In their new home they learned to trust that their parents would provide another meal and they wouldn't have to fight for scraps.

In other words, they didn't just *know* adoption; they experienced it, and it transformed them.

It's not enough for you and me to know our legal status as adopted children of God; we need to feel this truth in our hearts so that it affects the way we live. The Spirit's work is to bring us assurance of the Father's love.

- **We can have assurance of his love:** We will grow in our ability to put aside our anxieties and trust our Father to provide.
- **We can have assurance of his presence:** God is listening, watching, caring. Many a parent creeps into their child's room at night to check on their sleeping child. The child isn't aware, but the parent is always looking out for them.
- **We can have assurance of access to God:** Healthy children have no great sense of decorum. If they wake in the morning, they enter their parents' bedroom. They don't knock and wait; they just run right in.
- **We can have assurance of our inheritance:** A child is not a slave that can get fired. We will inherit with our older brother, Jesus.

So you are no longer a slave, but God's child; and since you are his child, God has made you also an heir.
(Galatians 4 v 7)

Paul concludes his paragraph by reminding the church that they're no longer slaves but God's children and heirs. Those are two very different ways of living the Christian life. Here are a couple of examples:

1. **Forgiveness.** Someone is incredibly rude to you. They snub you and belittle you in front of others. If we live as slaves, we have fragile identities and are anxious about our status—so we retaliate in anger. But if we are confident children of God, we can think, "I'm

secure in the Father's love. This person clearly isn't, so I forgive them and will pray for them."

2. **Lying.** Imagine you forget the birthday of someone significant—a spouse or sibling. No card is sent, no phone call made. If we live as slaves, we lie to cover it up because we worry about what they will think of us. "Err... It must have been eaten by the postman's dog," we suggest. But if we are confident children of God, we can be honest and say, "I'm so sorry, I forgot". We can admit our failure because we're confident that we're secure in our Father's love.

I'm not pretending that things are always this black and white. Yet here is the difference that comes when we know in our hearts—and live out the truth—that we have an unbreakable status as adopted children of God.

God is a Father who has loved us before the creation of the world so that he sent his Son to redeem us, justify us and grant us the status of his beloved children. His love is not begrudging; it is overflowing.

As God's children, we can never ever lose his love for us. *Will you allow this wonderful truth to change your heart?*

4. Does God's love for me vary?

As a young Christian, I heard the same phrase over and over: *"There's nothing you can do to make God love you more—and there's nothing you can do to make him love you less"*.

I thought it was helpful, as, by nature, all of us tend to think we earn God's favour. Yet, some questions niggled away in my head:

Q: Does God's love for me *really* not vary?

Q: Wouldn't he be more delighted with me if I used my evenings to tell people about Jesus than if I spent every night paying for time with prostitutes?

Q: Is there *nothing* I can do to make God love me more? Wouldn't he be more delighted with me if I gave away 50% of my income?

Certain verses didn't seem to fit very easily into the idea of our behaviour having no impact upon how God views us. For example, what do we do with the following (italics mine):

While he was still speaking, a bright cloud covered them, and a voice from the cloud said, "This is my Son, whom I love; with him *I am well pleased*. Listen to him!" (Matthew 17 v 5)

I will praise God's name in song
    and glorify him with thanksgiving.
This will *please the LORD more* than an ox,
    more than a bull with its horns and hooves.
(Psalm 69 v 30-31)

These are the ones *I look on with favour*:
    those who are humble and contrite in spirit,
    and who tremble at my word. (Isaiah 66 v 2)

For you were once darkness, but now you are light in the Lord. Live as children of light (for the fruit of the light consists in all goodness, righteousness and truth) and find out what *pleases the Lord*. (Ephesians 5 v 8-10)

 On the contrary, we speak as those approved by God to be entrusted with the gospel. We are not trying *to please people but God*, who tests our hearts.
(1 Thessalonians 2 v 4)

As we see in these verses:

- Jesus was God's perfectly loved Son. He is *the Son*. Yet it was still possible for him to do things that pleased his Father further.
- Old Testament believers could cause God greater pleasure through their thanksgiving—and by their humility before his word.
- Paul commands us in the New Testament to discover and live out what pleases God. That's certainly what he was trying to do.

Even with a brief glance, it appears that the Bible states there are things we can do that cause the Lord greater or lesser pleasure with us. So, how do we fit this together with his unconditional love? We need to distinguish between our unchanging *status* and our variable *walk* before God.

OUR STATUS BEFORE GOD	Our walk with God
UNCONDITIONAL	Conditional
FATHER'S LOVE FOR US	Father's pleasure with us or displeasure

With a few possible exceptions, the Bible doesn't talk of God's love for us varying. His love is unconditional because we are united to Christ. **But** his pleasure or displeasure with believers can vary widely. Whether we please him or grieve him *is conditional* upon our obedience.

Most parents know this intuitively (although imperfectly in most families). You might envisage this conversation playing out, late one evening:

Child: *(shouting)* "I hate you and I won't go to bed!"

Parents: "We're very disappointed with you. Unless you go to bed, you'll lose all screen time for the next two days." *(not shouting... well, maybe parents do... sometimes)*

Child: "What's happened to you? You're clearly upset with me. You no longer love me like you used to."

Parents: "We love you unconditionally. Because we love you, we want you to get a good amount of sleep. We also want you to learn obedience growing up. Right now you're not feeling our love, even though it's consistent. Right now you're experiencing our disappointment and frustration."

Would you say that nothing your child does can make you love them more or less? Probably. But great parents still feel disappointment and grief in their kid's behaviour.

God is the perfect Father, and we can both grieve him and cause him pleasure, even while his love is unchanging.

Let's look at Paul's prayer for the Colossian believers in Colossians 1. It's a lovely prayer and asks that they "may live a life worthy of the Lord and please him in every way: bearing fruit in every good work" (v 10).

In other words, it's possible to be a Christian living a life that is unworthy and displeasing **or** a life that is worthy and pleasing.

> 9 For this reason, since the day we heard about you, we have not stopped praying for you. We continually ask God to fill you with the knowledge of his will through all the wisdom and understanding that the Spirit gives, 10 so that you may live a life worthy of the Lord and please him in every way: bearing fruit in every good work, growing in the knowledge of God, 11 being strengthened with all power according to his glorious might so that you may have great endurance and patience, 12 and giving joyful thanks to the Father, who has qualified you to share in the inheritance of his holy people in the kingdom of light. 13 For he has rescued us from the dominion of darkness and brought us into the kingdom of the Son he loves, in whom we have redemption, the forgiveness of sins. (Colossians 1 v 9-13)

Christians are always loved by their Father

Before we get into the detail, let's remind ourselves that it's the knowledge of our *status* before the Lord that must help shape our *walk* with him. We need to have these things in the right order.

Here in Paul's prayer, he's clear that Christians have a status that can never change. Verse 12 says the Father **has** qualified you to share in his inheritance in the kingdom of light.

That's past tense. He **has** qualified you. The whole letter of Colossians is written to encourage the Christians that they don't lack anything. *They are already qualified by Jesus.*

A few months after David Bowie died in January 2016, his will was published. It was lovely to see that he'd given £1.4 million to a woman called Corinne Schwab. For 40 years she was his PA, running around and organising his life. Whatever he might be lacking, she found it and provided it. She earned herself an inheritance. Bowie recognised his debt to her and awarded her £1.4 million.

But the singer's two kids received £15 million each. A lot more! They'd never worked for him—never ran around serving him or got him out of a scrape. They'd done nothing to earn an inheritance. Their dad had qualified them himself. He gave life to them, raised them and educated them. He gave them everything.

Similarly, God the Father has qualified us to inherit. It's not our work and we don't deserve our inheritance. It's merely due to the work of Jesus that we are qualified and so will inherit with Christ, our older brother. How wonderful!

So, before we consider how we may bring pleasure or grief to God, let's remember that we've never been worthy of the Father's love, but he has bestowed it upon us anyway.

That's a truth that can easily become neglected or sidelined when we talk about pleasing the Lord.

The writer, J. I. Packer, makes a great point on this from Luke 15. In the story of the prodigal son, the foolish younger brother eventually recognises that he needs to go home. As he feeds pigs in a sty, he sees that his dad's hired staff have better living conditions than him. So he resolves to return.

On the journey home, he plans the speech he'll make: "I am no longer worthy to be called your son; make me like one of your hired servants" (Luke 15 v 19).

But before the son says anything, the father runs to him and hugs him. The son makes his speech: "I am no longer worthy to be called your son"—but the father ignores him, orders him to be clothed properly, and throws a party.

Packer makes the point that many Christians think like the younger brother. They become aware of their sin and think, "I am no longer worthy to be a Christian". But this is a complete failure to understand God's generosity and grace. We were *never* worthy to be called his children, and we will never do enough to earn the right to be his children. **But** he has given us that status. He has declared us worthy.

I think many of us think more about how our actions please or displease the Lord than we do about his unfailing love. But it's his love for us that must come first in our thinking.

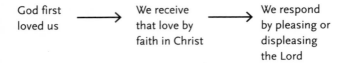

Bringing pleasure

Christians can bring both pleasure and grief to their Father. Paul's prayer in Colossians 1 is for growth. It begins with God—*"We continually ask God to fill you"* (v 9)—and his purpose is that believers might live a life worthy of the Lord and please him in every way.

Paul expands on that in four ways:

- bearing fruit in every good work (v 10)
- growing in the knowledge of God (v 10)

- being strengthened with power to endure (v 11)
- giving joyful thanks to the Father (v 12)

These four will put a smile on the face of the living God. But it's not an exhaustive list. There are all sorts of ways we can bring pleasure to the Lord:

> So we make it our goal to please him, whether we are at home in the body or away from it. [*faithful ministry*] (2 Corinthians 5 v 9)

> Children, obey your parents in everything, for this pleases the Lord. [*obedience*] (Colossians 3 v 20)

> I have received from Epaphroditus the gifts you sent. They are a fragrant offering, an acceptable sacrifice, pleasing to God. [*giving*] (Philippians 4 v 18)

> As for other matters, brothers and sisters, we instructed you how to live in order to please God, as in fact you are living. Now we ask you and urge you in the Lord Jesus to do this more and more. [*sexual morality*] (1 Thessalonians 4 v 1)

> And do not forget to do good and to share with others, for with such sacrifices God is pleased. (Hebrews 13 v 16)

While this is not a complete list, it's clear that there is a way of living as a Christian that brings pleasure to our heavenly Father.

One objection I've heard countless times is a clumsy quoting from Isaiah 64:

> All our righteous acts are like filthy rags. (Isaiah 64 v 6)

The argument runs, "See! The Bible insists that even our best actions are filthy. They're like sanitary towels before the Lord. Even the best deeds you do are unacceptable to God."

But Isaiah 64 is talking about Old Covenant believers recognising that their own actions cannot save themselves (64 v 5). That's true! If you think your own obedience *makes you righteous* that's offensive to God. But for the Christian believer, their good works or "righteous acts" can be entirely acceptable to God because we are "in Christ". We need to make this distinction:

- If you think your obedience *earns* God's love, that's offensive and filthy before him.
- If you view your obedience as a joy because God is good and you love him, your actions are a joy and a delight to him. They bring him pleasure.

Imagine a generous parent buys his 18-year-old daughter a brand new car. It's a free gift, with no strings attached. It wasn't even her birthday.

The following week, the dad says, "Darling, could you help me with an hour's gardening?"

She grumpily agrees but afterwards declares, "I hated that; I really don't enjoy your company. But now that I've spent one hour gardening, I've earned that car you gave me. I no longer feel indebted to you."

"What?!" her dad responds. "The car cost £15,000. You think one hour's work pays for that? I gave you the car because I love you. To be honest, it's pretty offensive that you can't accept it as a gift and you think a tiny bit of weeding can pay me off. I find your attitude filthy."

It would be very different if, when asked to help, the daughter immediately replied, "Sure Dad, of course. I love you. I love working with you. If you have something for me to do, I'll happily do it. It's my pleasure to help you out." The dad smiles as he thinks, "My girl brings me great delight!"

The difference is huge. A filthy act is one where there's no love—but rather an assumption that the car can be earned. But the act that pleases the father is one that flows out of their relationship.

So we need to be careful not to apply Isaiah 64 v 6 to all Christians. It's surely offensive to God to tell him that the good works he *planned* for us to do (Ephesians 2 v 10) are filthy! It's offensive to tell God that the fruit of his Spirit in our lives is rotten.

So, Christians *can* please God their Father with their actions. We should always make it our goal to please the Lord. Isn't that wonderful! What a breathtaking privilege that, despite our sin, the Bible insists that our actions can bring God pleasure. How encouraging!

Bringing grief or displeasure

The letters of the New Testament contain plenty of rebukes for believers doing things wrong, but we're also specifically told of God's displeasure:

> And do not grieve the Holy Spirit of God, with whom you were sealed for the day of redemption. (Ephesians 4 v 30)

> And have you completely forgotten this word of encouragement that addresses you as a father addresses his son? It says, "My son, do not make light of the Lord's discipline, and do not lose heart when he rebukes you." (Hebrews 12 v 5)

> I know your deeds, that you are neither cold nor hot. I wish you were either one or the other! So, because you are lukewarm—neither hot nor cold—I am about to spit you out of my mouth. (Revelation 3 v 15-16)

Believers can grieve the Spirit, earn a rebuke from the Father, and know the clear frustration of the risen Son. In lazy but normal language, *we can make God unhappy with us.*

Ephesians 4 v 17-32 shows us some of the behaviour that grieves the Spirit (v 30):

- sexual impurity and greed (v 19)
- lying (v 25)
- sinful anger (v 26)
- stealing, and failing to share your plenty with others (v 28)
- unwholesome and critical talk (v 29)
- bitterness, rage, anger, brawling, slander, malice (v 31)

It's true that a Christian can never lose God's love for them. That's wonderfully and deeply true. Yet the Bible talks about God's delight in the obedience of his children and his anger towards their disobedience.

He is such a wonderful Father that it's natural to aspire to please him. Of course we make mistakes, but then we return to him with repentance and know his forgiveness once again.

God isn't merely a satisfied judge, content with our status—he is also intimately involved in our lives and cares about our daily walk.

He's not a distant judge who is purely on our side legally because of Jesus.

He's not a naïve parent who dotes upon us regardless of our behaviour.

He's the perfect Father, whose love is unfailing. Yet he can still be grieved or pleased.

We can only please God because Jesus did (and we're united to him)

Paul's beautiful prayer in Colossians 1 concludes with his normal clear reference to Christians being "in him"—"the Son ... *in whom* we have redemption, the forgiveness of sins" (v 14). All the blessings of the Christian life come because we are united to Jesus. Here, it's through our union with the Son that we have redemption and forgiveness of sins.

> 12 [G]iving joyful thanks to the Father, who has qualified you to share in the inheritance of his holy people in the kingdom of light. 13 For he has rescued us from the dominion of darkness and brought us into the kingdom of the Son he loves, 14 in whom we have redemption, the forgiveness of sins. (Colossians 1 v 12-14)

Think of a British man who, on his travels overseas, meets and genuinely falls in love with an Iranian Christian woman. They marry and move back to the UK. She's now qualified to live in Britain and receive the benefits of life here because she is united to him. "In him" she has the benefits of a UK citizen, even though there's nothing about her that merits such benefits. Were he to tragically die, she would lose her right to remain. Her qualification to live in the UK depends entirely upon him.

That's true of our status before the Lord and our ability to please him. The reason you and I can live in a way that pleases God is because we're "in Jesus". It's true that even our best actions will be done with mixed motives. We care for someone who is sick—that's a great thing to do, but a little part of us hopes that others notice. We help others at church by leading Bible studies—but there's a little part of us that feels proud in our ability.

We'll never act with 100% pure motives this side of heaven, but it's okay. The muck of our motives is covered by Jesus. We can please God because we are united to Christ and his perfection. Peter is crystal clear on this, as is the writer to the Hebrews:

> You also, like living stones, are being built into a spiritual house to be a holy priesthood, offering spiritual sacrifices acceptable to God through Jesus Christ.
> (1 Peter 2 v 5)

> Now may the God of peace ... equip you with everything good for doing his will, and may he work in us what is pleasing to him, through Jesus Christ, to whom be glory for ever and ever. (Hebrews 13 v 20-21)

Our sacrifices are acceptable, and we can act in a way pleasing to God "*through* Jesus Christ".

It's wonderfully true that, by God's grace, there is nothing I can do to make God love me more or less. The status of righteous, adopted and loved is a permanent one, unaffected by my varying mood and behaviour. Yet, I can live a life that pleases God or grieves him. As I become more and more like Jesus, God takes greater and greater pleasure in me. This remains a work of his grace. It's achieved not in my own strength but by God's Spirit and because I'm united to the Son. So, let's pray the words of Hebrews 13, asking God that he will equip us with everything we need to do his will, and so bring him pleasure.

Does God's love for me vary?

Wonderfully the answer is no. Yet his pleasure or displeasure can vary.

As a colleague said to me recently, "I love my three-year-old very much; I always will. But when he shares his toys with his younger brother, I feel so pleased!"

Our God is a perfect Father with unfailing love for his believing children. Knowing that, let's practically do all we can to bring him pleasure. We've already mentioned some ways we can do this but let me add slightly to that list. Here are some of the unremarkable aspects of Christian living which are explicitly said to please the Lord:

- Trusting him rather than our own strength and abilities (Psalm 147 v 10-11)
- Giving money sacrificially (Philippians 4 v 18)
- Being pure sexually (1 Thessalonians 4 v 1-5)
- Giving time to others and sharing with them (Hebrews 13 v 16)
- Growing in knowledge of God (Colossians 1 v 10)
- Giving thanks joyfully (Colossians 1 v 12)
- Taking care of your family's practical needs (1 Timothy 5 v 4)
- Obeying his commands (1 John 3 v 22). That's a very broad one!

How wonderful that, despite our ongoing sin, we have the certainty of God's constant love **and** the ability to put a smile on his face with how we behave.

5. Will God still love me if I never obey him?

Robert Wringhim is a character in the novel *The Private Memoirs and Confessions of a Justified Sinner*. Robert grows up in a family that stresses how wonderful it is to be justified, but with no concept of grieving the Lord with our sin. Robert believes his behaviour can never make a difference: "How delightful to think that a justified person can do no wrong". He believes it's impossible for a believer to do anything to displease God—and eventually takes this to an extreme by murdering his brother.

That's nuts! It's a work of fiction, but the book's author, Robert Hogg, was commenting on his perception of Christianity in Scotland in 1824. Whether Hogg's opinion was fair or not, I don't know. But I do know we need to hold on to a balance in what the Bible teaches.

We've seen the wonderful confidence we can have as Christians. We have the unshakeable and unconditional status of being justified and therefore acceptable before God. It's a right standing by faith and not by works. So, in the previous chapter we said that, although Christians can please or displease their heavenly Father, we can never lose his love.

So what are we to make of Bible verses like these:

> What good is it, my brothers and sisters, if someone claims to have faith but has no deeds? Can such faith save them? (James 2 v 14)

> Whoever says, "I know him," but does not do what he commands is a liar, and the truth is not in that person. (1 John 2 v 4)

> God "will repay each person according to what they have done." To those who by persistence in doing good seek glory, honour and immortality, he will give eternal life. (Romans 2 v 6-7)

James says that a faith without works cannot save. **John** states that a failure to obey God makes any claim to faith a lie. **Paul** is clear that God will judge us according to our behaviour.

How does all this fit with an unconditional status of being right with God?

OUR STATUS BEFORE GOD	Our walk with God
UNCONDITIONAL—WON BY JESUS	Conditional—we're involved
SAVED WITHOUT ANY GOOD WORKS	Good works reveal that we are saved
WE CONTRIBUTE NOTHING TO OUR STATUS	Our actions demonstrate our status
JESUS' COMPLETED WORK FOR US	Jesus' ongoing work in us

For centuries Christians have summarised the Bible's teaching by saying, "We are saved by faith alone, but the faith that saves is never alone".

So, a response to the question in the chapter's title is this: *If you never obey God, are you really a believer?* Believers love to obey their Father. They struggle, get it wrong, and disobey at times, but at heart they want to obey him.

True faith is seen in action

The warnings in James 2 v 14 and 1 John 2 v 4 are against those who merely *say* they believe the gospel. Declaring that you believe in Jesus is not the same thing as saving faith. During the Reformation, faith came to be defined as:

1. knowledge,
2. belief, and
3. trust.

You might know what the Bible says about Jesus—good. You may then agree that it's true—great. But do you then trust Jesus? The Puritans had a fun word to describe faith: "recumbency". It means to lean against or lie down on something. I think the only way we still use the word is for recumbent pedal bikes— those bikes that look a bit dangerous as you lie flat to cycle them.

The Puritans meant that saving faith lies upon Jesus. It puts it weight upon Jesus. If you're at the top of a 20-storey building and lean upon the viewing rail, you're placing your weight upon it, trusting it can support you and will not let you fall.

That's one step beyond knowledge and belief. James puts it vividly:

> You believe that there is one God. Good! Even the
> demons believe that—and shudder. You foolish person,
> do you want evidence that faith without deeds is
> useless? (James 2 v 19-20)

The demons have knowledge of God; they believe in his existence, but they do not trust him. They are not "recumbent" upon him (love that word). There's a difference between intellectual assent and trust. We get that; we see it in everyday life.

I have a terrible sense of direction. When the Lord gave out gifts, navigation wasn't one of mine. My wife is far, far better. A couple of years ago, our family had a great holiday in the south of France. On the drive back to the UK, our sat nav told us there was an accident on the Paris ring road and suggested an alternative route. We seemed to be driving through the centre of Paris, but okay, we'd trust the sat nav. But then it flipped out and went haywire. Hmm, the centre of Paris with no sat nav and no map...

"No problem," I informed the family. "I've driven in Paris before; we'll work it out." We were soon lost. My wife jumped out, bought a map, sat back down and said, "Right, do you trust me? If so, do as I say."

At that point my trust or faith was clearly demonstrated in my deeds. I couldn't sensibly say, "I do trust you but when you say left, I prefer to go right". My obedience to my wife's commands demonstrated my faith.

To push the illustration beyond the events, if I'd failed to listen to my wife's instructions—say I'd panicked and gone the wrong way, or had a stubborn moment and ignored her—at that point my faith or trust in her would have been seen in repenting. I'd have said "sorry", turned around and done what she said.

That's an illustration of a "saving faith". Not just accepting that my wife is correct, but listening to her and doing what she says. That's what James is describing. We cannot sensibly say, "I do trust you Jesus, but when you say, 'Follow me', I prefer to go in the other direction".

James' comments are consistent with the whole of the New Testament.

Paul evens wraps the book of Romans in this truth (italics mine):

> Through him we received grace and apostleship to call
> all the Gentiles to *the obedience that comes from faith* for
> his name's sake. (Romans 1 v 5)

> ... so that all the Gentiles might come to *the obedience
> that comes from faith.* (Romans 16 v 26)

"The obedience that comes from faith" is more literally translated as "the obedience of faith". In his commentary on Romans, Christopher Ash helpfully summarises this as *"bowing the knee in trusting submission to Jesus the Lord, both at the start and in the continuation of the Christian life"*.

Or to use another word, faith is ongoing *recumbency* upon Jesus. (Okay, that's the last time.)

True faith changes you

The best news of the gospel is the new status we're given. In Jesus we are righteous (in right standing with God) and therefore have a right to eternal life, and are loved by the Father as adopted sons. That status will last for eternity.

Yet salvation is not *merely* a legal verdict upon us. When we become Christians, Jesus changes us. That's also brilliant news. It would be tragic if we viewed living a transformed life as a burden. We are united to him and he is at work in us to make us more like him. This is great news! In a wonderfully encouraging verse, Paul tells the believers in Corinth:

> We ... are being transformed into his image with ever-
> increasing glory, which comes from the Lord, who is the
> Spirit. (2 Corinthians 3 v 18)

That's normal Christian living. The New Testament doesn't conceive of salvation without a transformed life. It has no category for the genuine believer who does not grow in holiness.

I think of a woman from church who I'll call Carol. She moved to London aged 22 and shortly afterwards became a Christian. A few weeks later she met with her old college mates who declared, "It's time to get lashed!" But after a few drinks, Carol stopped and just drank cola. "What's this?" her friends asked. "That's not the old Carol talking." She was brave enough to say, "You're right. I'm a new Carol since becoming a Christian. I'm here to have fun but, unlike in the past, fun without regrets the next day."

She recognised that she didn't have to and didn't want to live the same way as before. She was united to Christ, with a new desire to live for him.

A saving faith in Jesus Christ means you're never the same.

What we do reveals the reality of our faith

Let's put two verses of Scripture next to one another, to be absolutely sure we get what they're saying:

> [I am] found in him, not having a righteousness of my own that comes from the law, but that which is through faith in Christ—the righteousness that comes from God on the basis of faith. (Philippians 3 v 9)

> You see that a person is considered righteous by what they do and not by faith alone. (James 2 v 24)

If we sat Paul and James down in the same room and asked what they meant, the answer would be:

- **Paul:** *You are saved apart from works* = you are saved apart from the **merit** of works.

- **James:** *You cannot be saved apart from works* = you cannot be saved apart from the **presence** of works.

Paul was anxious that no one thought their actions could make them right with God. James was anxious that no one thought being a Christian could leave you unchanged.

The works (the things we do) do not contribute to our righteousness (we cannot earn a right standing with God), but they do reveal that we are united to him and that he is changing us. Jesus gives his own great illustration of this in John 15:

> "I am the vine; you are the branches. If you remain in me and I in you, you will bear much fruit; apart from me you can do nothing." (John 15 v 5)

Jesus calls us "branches", which are united to him who gives life and therefore bearing fruit.

1. If we ask, "What makes the branch alive, the vine or the fruit?" the answer is obvious: it's the vine. Any branch, sawn off, will produce nothing.
2. But if we ask, "How can you tell if the branch is alive?" the easiest way to do so quickly is to ask, "Is it bearing fruit?"

So for the Christian:

1. What makes us alive and righteous before God? It is faith in Jesus that unites us to him, the source of life.
2. How can you tell if someone is a Christian? One easy way is to ask, "Are they bearing fruit in godly living?"

Look to Jesus, and not yourself

It's good to get these things clear in our minds. Our lives need to show fruit that reveals that our faith in Christ is real.

James is concerned that we don't divorce our justification from our transformation as Christians. They both come when we're united to Jesus. Yet Paul remains anxious that we don't blur our justification and our transformation. That would lead us to think we contribute to our righteousness (our right standing before God). We do not.

Something we do for God can be described as a sweet smelling aroma to the Lord (Philippians 4 v 18) if we do it out of love for him. But if we think it contributes to our righteousness, then Paul would describe the same activity as garbage (literally *dung*) in God's sight (Philippians 3 v 8).

When I stand in God's courtroom and await the verbal declaration of being righteous, I will have no confidence in my achievements. I will have no confidence in my good works. I will have no confidence in how much I have changed. My confidence before the Lord is that I have righteousness by faith in Christ.

There's a reason why, for decades, Christians have enjoyed singing Toplady's hymn, "Rock of Ages". It expresses clearly where our confidence lies:

Nothing in my hand I bring,
Simply to thy cross I cling;
Naked, come to thee for dress;
Helpless, look to thee for grace;
Foul, I to the fountain fly;
Wash me, Saviour, or I die!

So, don't become a navel-gazer, always anxious about your obedience. Look to Jesus for your righteousness and allow him to change you so that your life reveals your faith. And just because we've talked about the need for a life that reveals our faith, don't start looking at yourself obsessively. *Keep looking to Christ.*

6. Should I ever feel guilty?

"Guilt is a wasted emotion."
That was the headline in an article someone passed me. (It was from *Psychology Today*, which really isn't my regular reading.) The sub-heading gave the reason: "Don't get caught up in others' judgments about you."

That's a common headline today. Our culture tells us not to worry about what others think of us. We should never feel guilty as long as we act in a way that's true to ourselves. I can imagine this has helped some people weighed down with excessive guilt, but I suggest it's largely twaddle.

We've been looking at our objective status before God. We may please or displease the Lord, but our status cannot change: his love for us is unconditional in Christ. Yet, how should we *feel* when we sin? Should we ever feel guilty? It's helpful to return to our chart.

OUR STATUS BEFORE GOD	Our walk with God
UNCHANGING	Changeable
UNCONDITIONAL	Conditional
FATHER'S LOVE FOR US	Father's pleasure with us or displeasure
FORGIVEN	Fluctuating guilt / forgiveness

Sometimes we find ourselves asking questions like this:

Q: If Christians are forgiven once and for all, why do we confess our sins? Hasn't Jesus already paid for them?

Q: What happens if I don't confess sin, on a Sunday or personally day by day? Are those sins not forgiven?

Q: Even if my status before God doesn't change, should I go though an emotional cycle of guilt and relief?

Let's look at two sections of Scripture to help us get our thinking clearer and keep guilt in its right place. First is the wonderful Psalm 32.

¹ Blessed is the one
> whose transgressions are forgiven,
> whose sins are covered.

² Blessed is the one
> whose sin the LORD does not count against them
> and in whose spirit is no deceit.

³ When I kept silent,
> my bones wasted away
> through my groaning all day long.

⁴ For day and night
> your hand was heavy on me;
> my strength was sapped
> as in the heat of summer.

⁵ Then I acknowledged my sin to you
　　and did not cover up my iniquity.
　I said, "I will confess
　　my transgressions to the LORD."
　And you forgave
　　the guilt of my sin.

⁶ Therefore let all the faithful pray to you
　　while you may be found;
　surely the rising of the mighty waters
　　will not reach them.
⁷ You are my hiding place;
　　you will protect me from trouble
　　and surround me with songs of deliverance.

⁸ I will instruct you and teach you in the way you should go;
　　I will counsel you with my loving eye on you.
⁹ Do not be like the horse or the mule,
　　which have no understanding
　but must be controlled by bit and bridle
　　or they will not come to you.
¹⁰ Many are the woes of the wicked,
　　but the LORD'S unfailing love
　　surrounds the one who trusts in him.

¹¹ Rejoice in the LORD and be glad, you righteous;
　　sing, all you who are upright in heart! (Psalm 32 v 1-11)

Most commentators believe David wrote this psalm after he'd been exposed as having an adulterous affair with Bathsheba and ordering her husband, Uriah, to be murdered (2 Samuel 11 and 12). And yet David begins his psalm with absolute delight. He is *thrilled* to know forgiveness and that his relationship with God has been restored.

The focus in verses 1-2 is upon the Lord's forgiveness, but there is also a second blessing that David knows:

> "Blessed is the one whose sin the LORD does not count against them *and in whose spirit is no deceit*." (Psalm 32 v 2, italics mine)

David both knows the Lord's forgiveness *and* now can live without deceit or hypocrisy. His conscience is clear, and that's a wonderful thing. As Christians, we're not meant to live with overwhelming guilt. We're meant to take it to the cross of Jesus and know forgiveness.

Yet an awareness of guilt, and therefore deliberate confession, are important parts of Christian living too...

Guilt is good... if we're guilty

Sometimes it's good to feel guilty. Namely at those times when we've done something wrong! If I met a corrupt businessman who was stealing funds from his employees' pension fund, I'd hope he felt guilty. He might say, "Guilt is a wasted emotion. I want to be super-rich and so, in stealing money, I'm only being true to myself." I'd naturally reply, "To be honest, your staff would benefit from a colossal dollop of guilt in your conscience".

That's an unlikely example, but what about Christian believers. Are we ever guilty? Should we ever *feel* guilty?

Some Christians will say, "Don't be introspective. Don't criticise your own life. You'll be forgiven whatever you do, so don't go looking for faults!" Yet sometimes we do need to.

Take the example of John Newton, the hymn-writer, who was converted while a slave trader. That was and remains a despicable profession: kidnapping humans and transporting them in appalling squalor and suffering to sell them as property. It's horrible. John Newton became a Christian and... carried on as a slave trader for a few more years.

Isn't it good that after a while he began to feel guilty about his profession? Wouldn't he ideally have felt guilty a little earlier?

In the 21st century, Newton might have read in *Psychology Today* that "guilt is a wasted emotion". But, not when you're guilty. Newton felt guilty over what he was doing and made a change. Good!

In Psalm 32 David describes how he felt when he was aware of his guilt but hadn't addressed it:

> When I kept silent, my bones wasted away through my groaning all day long. For day and night your hand was heavy on me; my strength was sapped as in the heat of summer. (Psalm 32 v 3-4)

Clearly his guilt had a huge emotional and physical impact. Though we might be surprised by the physical symptoms, they're not that unusual. Plenty of us have known the impact that stress can take on our bodies, and how physically exhausted we can be after an emotionally intense period. Some of us may have known some echo of David's experience. When you're conscious that you've done something really wrong, then unconfessed sin is like a splinter in the soul. It just keeps niggling and irritating your conscience. It will not let you settle.

My wife got a little splinter in her finger on a Saturday afternoon. We were out in the evening and it was clearly niggling her. She kept rubbing her finger and trying to force the thing out. On some occasions, if you don't remove a splinter it can cause infection and (in admittedly very rare circumstances) can even cause organ damage.

Fortunately her heroic husband was able to address the situation on Sunday with the use of a pin and some tweezers!

The niggling pain a splinter produces is good. It means we address the issue before it becomes serious. A guilty conscience functions in the same way. It provokes us to address our sin before we become hardened to rebelling against God.

Confession brings comfort

> Then I acknowledged my sin to you and did not cover up
> my iniquity. I said, "I will confess my transgressions to
> the LORD." And you forgave the guilt of my sin.
> (Psalm 32 v 5)

Here's the turning point both of the psalm and in David's experience. He confessed his sin and the Lord forgave him. David is clear that he was "guilty". This is no mere self-pitying regret, but an admission that he was in trouble before God. We see from how the psalm continues that this clearly brought an enormous sense of relief.

A little while back a young man I know, who I'll call Adam, joined the staff team at a local church. Adam was very able, great with people and good at teaching the Bible. Yet he developed a certain melancholy. He began to let people down at short notice and became generally unreliable. Eventually he agreed with his boss that it wasn't really working and so he resigned. It was a surprise to everyone.

He married a couple of years later, but was distant in marriage and held himself back. Things weren't quite right. Eventually he confessed that two years prior to marriage, while he was working for the church, he'd been sexually active with multiple partners. He knew it was wrong, and he had felt guilty, but never confessed it. The hypocrisy had been eating away at him for years. It ruined his ministry and damaged his marriage. Eventually he was brought to a point of emotional collapse and everything poured out.

It was a really tough period for him but afterwards he rediscovered joy and the liberation of living free from guilt. He could say with David, "Blessed is the one whose transgressions are forgiven ... in whose spirit is no deceit".

That's a strong example, but any unconfessed sin can make us feel isolated from God and from others at church. We know we're living a lie. Wonderfully, confession brings relief as we know God's forgiveness and we feel that we belong again at church. We rejoin the ranks of joyful, forgiven sinners.

In a highly evocative phrase, the old Puritan writer Thomas Manton suggested that, "Confession is the vomit of the soul". We clear out things that initially tasted good but actually are poison to us. No one enjoys vomiting, but it can bring relief. Sometimes, having to confess to others what we've done is horrible but it brings sweet relief.

Question: Did God not forgive David until the moment of confession?

Verse 5 certainly reads that way: "Then I acknowledged my sin to you ... and you forgave the guilt of my sin".

Does this mean that when Christians sin, God does not forgive us until we confess? Do we lose our status as forgiven and then regain it after confession?

To put it as a picture, is it that Christians live in God's house, but when we sin we get kicked out and have to sit outside? And it's only when we confess that we're allowed back in? Is that the correct picture?

No.

Here again the difference between our status and our walk with God is key. Our status as forgiven does not change. There is no transaction that takes place when we confess our sins. *We never leave the house.*

Rather, when we confess our sin, that's how we **know** in our hearts and minds and emotions that we remain in God's love. Confession allows us *to enjoy living in God's house.* We don't feel the need to hide away in a bedroom because we're embarrassed to look our Father in the eye.

My friend, Christopher Ash, expresses it very well: "It is in my conscience that I hear God's gracious word of justification in Christ. I do not hear it outwardly and in theory; I hear it in my experience and self awareness."

When I was a 17-year-old, I had one friend, Peter, who my parents really didn't like. He was a lot older and always in trouble. One Friday night I told my mum and dad I was going to the cinema with Stuart. In fact I'd gone drinking with Peter.

I came back late, expecting everyone to be asleep. To my surprise, my dad was still up at midnight. "You lied to me," he said. "Stuart phoned for you this evening. Who were you with?" After I told him, he looked me firmly in the eye and slowly said, "Son... Do. Not. Lie. To. Me."

The next morning we'd planned that Dad would take me for a driving lesson. I assumed that would no longer happen, and so sheepishly made my way downstairs mid-morning. To my surprise, he said, "Hurry up or we won't have time for your lesson". I nervously responded, "I thought you'd still be angry with me". He smiled. "Yes, I was angry, but look at the garden. I've taken it out on the trees. Come on, let's go."

My father treated me with grace. I was at no stage thrown out of the house, and he even went out of his way to help me with driving. But I was aware of awkwardness between us.

It was at this point that I apologised properly to him for lying and we were able to enjoy the rest of the day. My memory isn't perfect, but to my recollection, I never knowingly lied to him again.

Honest confession matters

The Bible does not teach us that Christians move in and out of God's forgiveness. *We do not move in and out of God's house.* But some verses do seem to suggest that:

> [8] If we claim to be without sin, we deceive ourselves and the truth is not in us. [9] If we confess our sins, he is faithful and just and will forgive us our sins and purify us from all unrighteousness. (1 John 1 v 8-9)

Verse 9 *looks* as if God's forgiveness depends upon us making confession. But the contrast with verse 8 is important. John is writing against someone who "claims to be without sin". His point is that if you never confess your sin, you don't really understand the gospel and have never been a Christian. *You never really went into God's house.* You thought you did but you had the wrong address. The Christian is one who recognises that, as a principle, they need to confess their sins.

So that explains how John can also write this verse:

> I am writing to you, dear children, because your sins have been forgiven on account of his name. (1 John 2 v 12)

This verse is a good translation of a clear past tense in the original Greek language: your sins *have been* forgiven. It took place the moment you repented and were united to Jesus.

In 1 John 1 v 8-9, the contrast is between two people who both sin. One says, "No problem here, no forgiveness required". They cannot be a Christian. The second says, "I know I'm guilty and I need Jesus to forgive me". That's the Christian response.

In John Newton's most famous hymn he declared, "Amazing grace, how sweet the sound that saved a *wretch* like me". He never moved on from that self-awareness. At the age of 82, Newton said, "My memory is nearly gone, but I remember two things: that I am a great sinner and that Christ is a great Saviour".

1 John 1 v 8-9 is not saying we move in and out of God's forgiveness—but that the Christian is one who knows they remain sinful, and that Christ is the Saviour, who has won their status of forgiveness—a status that cannot change.

Practically speaking

Let me make two practical observations about the benefits of regular confession:

In church

Not all churches say or sing a corporate confession when they gather together. I think that's a mistake. There's nothing magical about the words, and some will complain that it's easy to say them without engaging your brain—I know that. Yet I think it's a very strange church meeting without any confession—and it's really *healthy* to have one.

Our own church gatherings are very informal, but we still use confessions written nearly 500 years ago by Thomas Cranmer, the English Reformer. We regularly say these words:

> *"We earnestly repent, and are truly sorry for all our misdoings. The memory of them grieves us. The burden of them is more than we can bear."*

Alongside confession, Cranmer always had a prayer of assurance—words such as:

"May almighty God, who sent his Son into the world to save sinners, bring you his pardon and peace, now and for ever. Amen."

I think that has an impact upon people. It helps us remember the same two things that John Newton did: we are great sinners and we need Christ, the great Saviour. It helps us hold together grief at sin and joy in the security of God's love. It reminds us that we are perfect in God's sight and yet still sinners.

If there's never any confession, Christian meetings can be little more than motivational gatherings that puff you up with pride. If there's confession, but no gospel encouragement, then people will leave convicted but glum. A healthy church confesses deeply and then rejoices in their forgiveness.

In our own personal prayers
Second, let me encourage you in the practice of regular confession in your own personal prayers. Again, it's so important for a healthy Christian life that joyfully clings to Jesus as a great Saviour.

A lack of confession leads to a hardening of the heart, a little like water freezing. When water first begins to freeze, it is feeble. Anything can fall through it and it's easily broken. Yet when cooled for long enough and left alone to freeze, water can become solid enough for humans to skate on it. It can withstand a sledgehammer.

Regular confession of sins, in our own private devotions, and perhaps to a good Christian friend, can be the warm air that prevents our hearts freezing hard. It keeps them tender and warm.

Often the easiest way to do this is to think through your previous day. Are you conscious of things you've done wrong? Name them; and then give thanks that where you failed, Jesus never did. You're united to your great Saviour and so God views you as perfect because of him.

When you read the Bible, does it bring conviction of where you fall short? Here again, confess your sin and rejoice in your Saviour.

It's when we think through our need for the gospel in the details of our lives that we have greater cause to sing with joy (even if your song is just quietly in your heart).

In Psalm 32, David's confession and awareness of forgiveness caused him to sing and to encourage others to do the same:

> "Rejoice in the LORD and be glad, you righteous; sing, all
> you who are upright in heart!" (Psalm 32 v 11)

Why not stop right now and confess your sins to the Lord? And then sing your joy!

7. Does God reward us differently?

I like rewards.

I like the fact that after nine flat whites, my favourite coffee shop rewards my loyalty with one free one. I enjoy the fact that when I use my credit card, I'm rewarded with air miles (I never seem to use them, but it still makes me feel good). So if I'm told I'll get a reward from God, I instinctively like it.

Yet...

That does seem at first glance to contradict *grace*. It doesn't sit easily with the idea of salvation being a gift that's completely undeserved.

Plenty of us get a bit jumpy about the idea of heavenly rewards. Perhaps we see it as a "dangerous doctrine" that could encourage us to a faith driven by our performance. We're not helped by our success-driven culture. Many of us experience competition in the workplace and anxiety over the quality of our work. Many parents feel pressure about the achievements of their children.

If we conceive of heavenly rewards like a bonus from a demanding boss, we're in trouble. We're likely to have a faith driven by anxious service of God. But the Bible encourages us to view heavenly rewards as gifts from our Father: a loving Father who has secured our place with him in the future, and has graciously equipped and enabled us to serve him in the present.

Imagine a young man, heir to his father's fortune of millions. He hasn't earned the fortune coming to him; he was merely born into it—and when his father dies he will inherit the whole estate. However, his dad is no fool and doesn't want to raise an idle child. He regularly encourages his son to study hard at school and to practise on his musical instruments. He promises the son that if he works hard and makes the most of his ability, then he will reward him with a new phone, a new car, or a holiday away with friends. The father does this to teach his son the value of hard work. The boy will inherit regardless, but the dad will use promises and rewards to ensure the son will lead a useful life.

God treats us in the same way. Even though eternal life is a gift of grace won by Jesus, he promises us heavenly rewards if we give our lives to serving him.

The purpose of rewards

Paul makes lots of references to heavenly rewards; perhaps he is clearest when he writes to the church in Corinth:

> Therefore judge nothing before the appointed time; wait until the Lord comes. He will bring to light what is hidden in darkness and will expose the motives of the heart. At that time each will receive their praise from God. (1 Corinthians 4 v 5)

⁹ So we make it our goal to please him, whether we are at home in the body or away from it. ¹⁰ For we must all appear before the judgment seat of Christ, so that each of us may receive what is due to us for the things done while in the body, whether good or bad.

(2 Corinthians 5 v 9-10)

I'm struck in 1 Corinthians 4 v 5 that *"each will receive their praise from God"*. That seems to indicate a clear difference between believers. We will not all receive the same praise, like the relentless, bland clapping of hands that parents are forced to continue for hours at a school prize day. It's not that we all receive the same praise, but that each receives their own.

Similarly in 5 v 10, every individual appears before the judgment seat of Christ to "receive what is due to us for the things done while in the body".

Paul encourages the Corinthians that how they live *now* matters for eternity—not in getting them into heaven, but in the reward they will receive. The purpose of rewards is **not** to make us feel unsettled about our status, but to spur us on as Christians to serve the Lord wholeheartedly.

Once again, as with other truths in this book, we can pull apart our place in heaven and our reward:

OUR STATUS BEFORE GOD	Our walk with God
UNCHANGING	Fluctuating
UNCONDITIONAL	Conditional
OUR PLACE IN HEAVEN	Our reward in heaven

What actually can we do to earn a reward?

Well, lots of things. Which is good. It's in the words of Jesus that we hear most about rewards. We can gather them up under various headings:

Choosing the praise of God *then* over the praise of men *now*

> "Blessed are you when people insult you, persecute you and falsely say all kinds of evil against you because of me. Rejoice and be glad, because great is your reward in heaven, for in the same way they persecuted the prophets who were before you." (Matthew 5 v 11-12)

You can choose to hide your allegiance to Jesus and know popularity now—or you can know persecution for Jesus' sake and be rewarded in heaven. Similarly in Matthew 6, when you give, pray and fast, you can either do so for the reward of worldly acclaim now, or do it for the reward of God's acclaim then (Matthew 6 v 1-6, 16-18). You cannot do both.

Again, later in Matthew, Jesus stresses loving him ahead of family:

> "And everyone who has left houses or brothers or sisters or father or mother or wife or children or fields for my sake will receive a hundred times as much and will inherit eternal life." (Matthew 19 v 29)

Being generous with your money and resources

In Luke 14, Jesus offers his dinner host a choice. He can invite for a meal people who will repay him now, or he can invite the poor.

> "Although they cannot repay you, you will be repaid at the resurrection of the righteous." (Luke 14 v 14)

Faithfulness to Jesus' ministry of saving the lost

> 9 Jesus said to him, "Today salvation has come to this house, because this man, too, is a son of Abraham. 10 For the Son of Man came to seek and to save the lost."

> [11] While they were listening to this, he went on to tell them a parable, because he was near Jerusalem and the people thought that the kingdom of God was going to appear at once. [12] He said: "A man of noble birth went to a distant country to have himself appointed king and then to return. [13] So he called ten of his servants and gave them ten minas. 'Put this money to work,' he said, 'until I come back.' [14] "But his subjects hated him and sent a delegation after him to say, 'We don't want this man to be our king.'" (Luke 19 v 9-14)

Jesus tells this parable to teach how believers should act while they are waiting for him to return. He gives one mina each to ten servants. To be clear, a mina is not a man who digs for coal, but a unit of money, about three months' wages. So it's quite a sum of money he entrusts to these individuals. On the UK national average wage, that's about £6500. Beyond that, Jesus highlights a few things:

1. This is a gift. The king gave it to them; they did not own it themselves.
2. He tells them to put it to work.
3. This is the work we do until Jesus returns.

What does that mean for us? Jesus has just said in verse 10 that "the Son of Man came to seek and to save the lost". That's the work of Jesus the King. Verse 11 reveals that Jesus tells this parable to people who thought he was going to reign as King immediately. He corrects them and tells them how they are to act while waiting for him to return after he has ascended to heaven. The Son of Man (a title Jesus often used for himself) came to seek and save the lost—that is his work—so it makes most sense to view the parable as being about the same thing. While we wait for Jesus to return, Christians should use their gifts and abilities to be about his work: seeking and saving the lost.

> [15] "He was made king, however, and returned home. Then he sent for the servants to whom he had given the money, in order to find out what they had gained with it. [16] "The first one came and said, 'Sir, your mina has earned ten more.' [17] " 'Well done, my good servant!' his master replied. 'Because you have been trustworthy in a very small matter, take charge of ten cities.' [18] "The second came and said, 'Sir, your mina has earned five more.' [19] "His master answered, 'You take charge of five cities.'" (Luke 19 v 15-19)

Jesus will one day return to claim his kingdom and will reward his people. We're meant to notice several things.

First, the rewards are crazily generous! The first servant did well. He was given £6,500 but he earned £65,000, which is good work. But his reward was ten cities. Wow! Of course cities vary in size. But even if it was only the ten smallest cities in the UK, you would still undoubtedly be a billionaire. The reward is completely out of proportion to the gift.

Second, the rewards here vary. Not everyone is given the same. Let me again stress that these are initially rewards of grace. Jesus is rewarding people for using the gifts he has given. Years ago, Augustine observed that when God gives rewards, "[God] is crowning his own gifts". No one in heaven will say, "I *deserve* my reward for my *efforts*". Rather, we will say, "God graciously enabled me to serve him, and then went further and rewarded me for the opportunity he gave".

Last, the basis upon which rewards are granted is for being *trustworthy*. That's what counts. We are to use the gifts Jesus gives us by putting them to work to seek and save the lost.

That's what secures a reward in this parable (and Matthew 25, which is similar). I think this is why Paul can describe converts as his joy and crown (1 Thessalonians 2 v 19; Philippians 4 v 1).

So a variety of behaviour in the New Testament is said to be worthy of a reward, but underpinning all of it is choosing to give our lives *now* for the good and growth of Jesus' kingdom.

What form do the rewards take?

Here again, we can be misled by worldly reward systems. I have a gold watch that my dad was given for 25 years service to his company. He sold fuel to farmers, so the watch really had nothing to do with his work. If we think of heavenly rewards as a sort of "gold watch", then we'll go wrong. Of course, the New Testament does speak in numerous places of winning a crown of gold, but that doesn't really help me either. I'm not much into bling, and I'm hoping for sunshine in the new creation, so a heavy, sweaty crown just isn't that appealing.

Of course, this is just a picture of being *honoured*.

With all the pictures the New Testament gives of rewards, we want to understand the reality to which they point. Yet, while that's what we may want, it's quite hard to do. It seems that the Lord gives us a variety of encouraging pictures of rewards so that we don't fixate on one thing.

So what pointers are we given?

Responsibility

In the parable of the minas above, the reward seems to take the form of responsibility (ten cities, five cities, etc.). That may or may not fill you with enthusiasm, but many of us do love work that is both challenging and yet within our capabilities.

The fulfilment of our earthly activity

We get another indication of the nature of rewards in the Beatitudes (Matthew 5 v 1-12), where Jesus clearly shows a connection between our behaviour now and our reward then:

> 5 Blessed are the meek, for they will inherit the earth.
> 6 Blessed are those who hunger and thirst for
> righteousness, for they will be filled.
> 7 Blessed are the merciful, for they will be shown mercy.
> 8 Blessed are the pure in heart, for they will see God.
> (Matthew 5 v 5-8)

Although these are the norms expected of every Christian, it does indicate that the rewards God gives are not random but connected to what we have done here on earth.

C. S. Lewis therefore compares our pursuit of heavenly rewards to a schoolboy learning a foreign language. Initially the boy learns French to get good marks in school; but in time he studies it because he loves the language. It means he can communicate freely in France and can read French literature. So the thing he did initially out of self-interest, he now does out of joy and because he appreciates the beauty and freedom of knowing the language.

In the same way, perhaps the desire for a reward motivates us in the beginning. But as we give ourselves to serving the Lord, we develop a deeper love for him that will be rewarded by *seeing* him (Matthew 5 v 8).

The praise of God

Our greatest reward is the acclaim of God that Jesus speaks of in Matthew 6, or the "Well done, good and faithful servant!" in Matthew 25. We long for "praise from God" (1 Corinthians 4 v 5).

Receiving praise from someone we respect is always great. I simply cannot fathom how wonderful it will be to look into the face of Jesus and hear him say to me, "Well done, my good servant!" At that moment, we'll be ecstatic with each and every decision we took to make a sacrifice for Jesus and to choose his praise over any other.

Common questions we ask

Q1: Is it okay to be motivated to godly living by the offer of a reward?

Yes! Because it's for God's glory, it's entirely appropriate to pursue a heavenly reward. It is indeed for our good, but Jesus commands us to live this way too. Wonderfully, Jesus is ordering us to pursue our own happiness by serving him wholeheartedly.

There would be something very odd and unhealthy if our *only* motivation for godliness was a reward. Instead, there are plenty of motivations for holy living in the New Testament:

- We are grateful for all that Jesus has done for us (Romans 12 v 1).
- We want to obey our Father because we love him and desire to please him (2 Timothy 2 v 15; Hebrews 13 v 16).
- We know that we've been set free from sin (Romans 6 v 11-12).
- We don't want to lead wasteful, unproductive lives (2 Peter 1 v 8).
- We long to see God honoured and know that our obedience brings him praise (2 Peter 3 v 18).

That's not an exhaustive list, but it's important to recognise that among the variety of motivations we're given for godliness, the concept of rewards is there. We would be foolish to deprive ourselves of an encouragement that Jesus gives.

Q2: Will I be jealous of others?

We are relentlessly proud and envious creatures here on earth, so it's hard for us to conceive of being in the new creation and being content that some people have a greater reward than us. We have a deep-rooted assumption within us that happiness is linked to our status and power!

Yet in a sinless world, there will be no jealousy, but only joy. It may trouble us now, but when we are all perfectly satisfied, there'll be no capacity for us to be unhappy.

The theologian Jonathan Edwards has a helpful picture of this. (Run with it, even though we've said that our reward is connected to our activity here on earth.) He tells us to imagine our rewards in heaven as boats launched upon an ocean of happiness. Every boat is absolutely full with satisfaction. Some boats are larger than others, but no one minds as everyone is on the ocean of happiness.

This picture works for me. I quite like sailing, and on a sunny day with good wind I'm entirely content sailing a small boat. I don't want a 40-foot yacht with loads of sails—that's a scary proposition.

Edwards makes one last point, derived from 1 Corinthians 12 v 26: "If one part [of the body] is honoured, every part rejoices with it". He suggests that those with smaller rewards will rejoice in the larger rewards of others. When we're no longer sinful, then we cannot be jealous—but we will be genuinely delighted when someone else is honoured.

Q3: Will we be proud of our achievements?

Nope, that would be daft. Every good work that we do, worthy of a reward, has been prepared in advance for us by God

(Ephesians 2 v 10), and we are utterly dependent upon the grace of God to do it. Our works *never* put God in our debt; he is under no obligation to reward us.

When I was a young boy, my father asked me to help him paint the garden fence with creosote. He promised me £5 for my labour. I was really far too young to be of any help but he didn't ask me because I would assist him. He asked me so that we would enjoy time together—and also he probably wanted to teach me that money comes through hard work (my dad was always trying to make this point to me!).

While he painted one fence panel, I would paint the one next to it. Two things became obvious. 1. He could paint four panels in the time I did one. 2. The way I painted was horrible, splotchy and uneven. When I declared that I'd finished a panel, Dad would come over, issue a "hmm, not bad", and then show me what a proper job looked like by completely redoing the panel. After a couple of panels, I suggested that I wasn't really helping and so perhaps should go inside and watch TV. He agreed.

Later on I asked hesitatingly if I'd earned my £5. Dad laughed, gave me the money, and told me I could have £5 more if I mowed the lawn (in our house that was a quick and easy five-minute job). He was being kind: rewarding me when I'd done little but get in his way, and yet encouraging me to keep on serving usefully.

He wasn't trying to make a theological point, but I've sometimes reflected that my hopeless actions as a child may well be like my actions as a Christian. God doesn't need my help. In fact I may well get in the way. Yet he calls me to serve him for the joy of working with him, and rewards me beyond what I deserve.

Yes, God kindly gives us abilities and a job to do in seeking the lost. Wonderfully he will reward us. But he is crowning his own gifts.

The Lord holds out the prospect of rewards in heaven as an encouragement to believers whose place there has been won by Jesus. It's a truth that should spur us on to make the most of our lives to serve the King.

There's no need to fear your place in heaven; that's a status won by Jesus.

There's no room for pride in your achievements—only joyful thanks.

And yet...

There's no point in wasting your life; your life *now* can secure a greater reward *then*.

7½. But does God *really* still love me?

7½?

Yep. Nothing new here. I'm not answering any further questions in this chapter. But having spent four chapters on how our walk with God can vary such a lot, there's a danger that some of us might start navel-gazing too much.

As we've seen, it's important to hold on to the possibility of grieving God, the necessity of good works, and the varying nature of rewards. But these truths must be built upon our unchanging status with God. It's that *status* that must drive and shape our *walk* with God. Too much introspection is unhelpful. As we saw in chapter two, sometimes we need to stop looking at our legs, and look instead at the solid ground upon which we stand—the work of Jesus.

Christians can never fall outside of the Father's love. It's impossible. So I think it's healthy to pause again on that truth before we go any further. One thing I've found personally helpful in the last few years is an old hymn of Charles Wesley:

"Weary of wandering from my God". It contains the truth of Romans 5 v 17 put into memorable verse:

O Jesus, full of truth and grace,
More full of grace than I of sin.

Isn't that great! There's always more grace for believers, no matter what they've done. There are periods when we need to know this deep in our hearts. To be honest, there have been times where I've repeated those lines over and over in my head until I actually believed them. There is more grace in Jesus than there is sin in me. Isn't that wonderful?

So Christian, God *really does* love you, despite your ongoing sin.

That's it.
That's what I wanted to say. Not really a chapter at all.
But... we'll take a brief look at Psalm 51 to try and rub that truth in.

If we want to celebrate our unchanging status as justified sinners, it can seem eccentric to turn to the Old Testament, where those truths are less clear than on this side of the cross and resurrection. Yet, for centuries, Psalm 51 has brought great comfort to believers, as we see David move from desperate appeal to joyful assurance.

Or to put it bluntly—if an adulterer and murderer who thought he could hide his crimes from God can still know the joy of being forgiven and living in God's presence, then so can you and I.

For the director of music. A psalm of David. When the prophet Nathan came to him after David had committed adultery with Bathsheba.

¹ Have mercy on me, O God,
    according to your unfailing love;
  according to your great compassion
    blot out my transgressions.
² Wash away all my iniquity
    and cleanse me from my sin. (Psalm 51 v 1-2)

A plea to be cleansed

The title of the psalm tells us that this is David's confession after Nathan the prophet had confronted him with God's message in 2 Samuel 12. To be precise, David isn't merely confessing his sin nor asking for forgiveness. *He's pleading for cleansing.* The three things David asks God for are:

- to blot out his transgressions (his deliberate rebellion),
- to wash away all his iniquity (his twisted corruption), and...
- to cleanse him from all his sin (his failure to hit the mark).

David recognises that there's a deep stain upon him. He compares himself to a foul garment that needs to be washed and cleansed again.

During my teenage years, I had a part-time job as a chef in a fish restaurant. After a 12-hour shift preparing and cooking fish, my chef's clothing stank! It took several cycles of the washing machine to get them looking and smelling clean again.

David feels that way before the Lord. But he doesn't just *feel* guilty—he has genuinely rebelled against his God. There is a legal record of crime that needs to be dealt with, and David knows that without that cleansing, he is unfit for the presence of God.

Wonderfully, David's awareness of the stain of sin upon him doesn't lead him to despair, because he knows the God to whom he draws near. Just as he asks for three things, David appeals to God on three terms, all of which Christians can see even more clearly, living this side of the cross. David appeals to:

- **God's mercy.** (Christians know that God is rich in mercy and raised us with Christ by grace, Ephesians 2 v 4-5.)
- **God's unfailing love.** (Christians know that nothing can separate us from the love of God that is in Christ Jesus our Lord, Romans 8 v 38-39.)
- **God's great compassion.** (Christians know the compassion of Christ as he sees helpless and harassed people, like sheep without a shepherd, Matthew 9 v 36.)

Isn't that a glorious combination? When we're afraid that our sin may have affected God's love for us Christians, then we need to remember his mercy, compassion and unfailing love.

But sometimes we forget and take these gifts for granted, so it's good to be brought to the point where we cry out and cherish God's love for us again. It's not a truth to leave gathering dust on a "mental mantelpiece". God's wonderful character is a truth that should affect us day by day.

When I was about eight, I went apple picking with my father. It's something we did every year with the permission of a local farmer. Dad would be 20 feet up on a ladder and throw down Bramley apples for me to catch and put in a crate. It was pretty good fun. But that year Dad must have overstretched and the ladder started to topple backwards towards me. Dad shouted at me to move but I was frozen stiff and did nothing. So rather than fall on top of me, he yanked at the ladder as it was falling and managed to spin it in a different direction. I was safe, but he landed badly on his back and cracked several vertebrae. He was lucky it was nothing worse, but still spent the next few weeks flat out in bed.

I vividly remember thinking, "Dad broke his back so that I wouldn't get hurt. He really does love me." It's not that I doubted it before. It's not that he became more vocal in expressing his love for me after this incident. Yet here was a vivid demonstration of a costly love.

Christians know that God loves them, but there are times when we are intensely conscious of our own sin and do start to doubt his love: "Perhaps he'll never love me quite the same," we wonder.

That's when we have to return to the cross and enjoy again the most vivid demonstration of his costly love. God in Christ was willing to bear his own wrath against sin. If we ask the question, "Does he really still love me?"—the answer is to look at God's mercy, compassion and unfailing love in Jesus Christ.

An awareness of sin

> ³ For I know my transgressions,
>   and my sin is always before me.
> ⁴ Against you, you only, have I sinned
>   and done what is evil in your sight;
>   so you are right in your verdict
>   and justified when you judge.
> ⁵ Surely I was sinful at birth,

sinful from the time my mother conceived me.
   ⁶ Yet you desired faithfulness even in the womb;
      you taught me wisdom in that secret place.
   (Psalm 51 v 3-6)

David refers to his sin eleven times in verses 1-9. He's not hiding from the fact that he has done wrong. Given that he has committed adultery (with Bathsheba) and murder (of Uriah), it's striking that he can tell the Lord, "Against you, you only, have I sinned". The focus here is on David's objective guilt before God. He's surely aware of the trouble he has caused on a human level, but here he's acknowledging the crime he has committed against his Maker. He goes further still. In verse 5, David acknowledges that he has always been sinful. He's a sinner through and through.

It's wonderfully liberating to admit to being a corrupt sinner who is still loved by the Lord. Yet some people struggle to do so. I can think of one friend who I'll call Trevor. Many years ago he went through a period of watching hardcore adult pornography online—the violent kind that is sometimes illegal. He confessed this to me as his pastor, as well as to his wife and good accountable friends. He consulted a friend who's a policeman to ask if he should report himself, but was told that it really wasn't significant enough for the police to follow up on. Yet despite this genuine confession, Trevor cannot believe that God has truly forgiven him.

As we've talked through this issue, it seems that Trevor struggles to believe that he's the kind of person who looks at abusive porn. He just can't believe he's that wretched. He's quite willing for Jesus to pay for the daily "small sins" of angry speech, selfish thoughts or unkind actions. But he really battles to come to terms with the depravity of his sin. He doesn't want to admit the depths of his iniquity. As a result,

Trevor cannot cast all of his sin upon Jesus, because he doesn't want to believe that he's so bad that he needs Jesus at such a deep level.

By contrast, David came to the point where he was greatly relieved to confess the fullness of his sin. There is wonderful relief in being honest with God about the worst of our sins. Here's the beautiful truth:

He knows it all already and he has paid for it all.

There's no perversion of ours that is hidden from the Lord. No depravity that will cause him to be surprised. No persistent deviance that he will be stunned by. He knows what pathetic failures we are.

We cannot out-sin Jesus' grace. We cannot commit offences beyond his ability to pay. He is more full of grace than we are of sin. Which means we can freely confess our sins and delight once again in Christ's forgiveness. In fact the Christian life should operate in a "virtuous spiral" a bit like this:

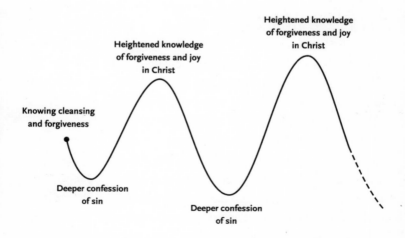

Confessing our sin and embracing Christ's forgiveness is wonderful. When we know that the worst of our offences can be forgiven, it permits deeper, honest reflection about who we really are. We're not limited to confessing obvious sins. We can allow God's word to convict us ever more deeply because we are utterly certain of more grace to come. That's what David comes to enjoy during this psalm. We're meant to confess sin with sincere regret but also wonderful relief. We despair at our transgressions, but also delight in God's forgiveness.

A return to joy and gladness

> [7] Cleanse me with hyssop, and I shall be clean;
>   wash me, and I shall be whiter than snow.
> [8] Let me hear joy and gladness;
>   let the bones you have crushed rejoice.
> [9] Hide your face from my sins
>   and blot out all my iniquity. (Psalm 51 v 7-9)

In verses 7-9, David is back to the appeal for cleansing. Hyssop was a bushy plant used like a brush to sprinkle sacrificial blood in Leviticus 14 and Numbers 19. Once someone was sprinkled with blood, they were pronounced clean. So the Christian reads these words and is reminded that, no matter what they've done, if they return in confession to the cross, they are sprinkled with the blood of Jesus and are clean.

Perhaps you'll find this a little silly, but for myself, every morning as I stumble groggily into the shower and allow the water to run over me, I give thanks that I start the day clean. Despite the failings of the day before, God's mercies are new every morning and, just as the water gushes over me to make me clean physically, so I know that Jesus' blood means I start the day clean spiritually. Wonderful.

David finds this is a cause for joy and gladness. Instead of feeling guilty and crushed, he rejoices. Instead of seeing himself as terribly stained, he knows he is whiter than snow.

While verses 1-9 are an appeal for cleansing, in the second half of the psalm David embraces being clean. The shift can be seen in the language he uses. Eleven times in verses 1-9 he addresses his sin, but only twice does he allude to it in verses 10-19. By contrast, David only names God once in verses 1-9, but six times in verses 10-19. He has looked at his sin realistically, but he has appealed to the God of mercy, compassion and unfailing love—and so he can look up at his God and look forward to being useful once more in his service.

> ¹² Restore to me the joy of your salvation
>
> > and grant me a willing spirit, to sustain me.
>
> ¹³ Then I will teach transgressors your ways,
>
> > so that sinners will turn back to you.
>
> ¹⁴ Deliver me from the guilt of bloodshed, O God,
>
> > you who are God my Saviour,
> >
> > and my tongue will sing of your righteousness.
>
> ¹⁵ Open my lips, Lord,
>
> > and my mouth will declare your praise.
>
> ¹⁶ You do not delight in sacrifice, or I would bring it;
>
> > you do not take pleasure in burnt offerings.
>
> ¹⁷ My sacrifice, O God, is a broken spirit;
>
> > a broken and contrite heart
> >
> > you, God, will not despise. (Psalm 51 v 12-17)

As a friend of mine puts it: *great sinners make great singers*. To know and to feel, like David, the deep-down weight and stain of your sin **and** to know and feel equally that you're forgiven through Jesus makes you a person who loves to sing of God's goodness in Christ. To sing literally, to speak to others, and to have a whole life that loves to sing about the Lord.

David fell spectacularly. Can you imagine how he would have answered if you had asked him some of the questions we've looked at over the last few chapters?

Q: David, do you think you've brought God pleasure?

Q: David, does your behaviour show that you're a believer in the Lord?

Q: David, are you expecting a reward for how you've behaved?

I think his responses when Nathan had exposed him would have been a shameful "No. No. And No."

And yet...

David knows the God who is merciful, compassionate and full of unfailing love. He trusts in the grace of God supremely seen in Jesus Christ. He confesses, receives cleansing, and so praises the Lord and serves him again.

David knew in shadow what we know even more clearly this side of the cross:

O Jesus, full of truth and grace,
More full of grace than I of sin.

8. Why is change so slow?

Recently, a man who I'll call Peter became a Christian at our church. He was in his mid-40s and an alcoholic. When he became a Christian, he declared his intention never to drink again and, to his wife's delight, for a while he did well. Then he started to stumble.

Peter worked from home one or two days a week, and on those days he could easily consume a twelve-pack of lager, a bottle of wine and maybe some spirits too. When work took him to a hotel for a couple of nights, he'd go on a similar binge. Peter became enormously discouraged. His wife was understandably upset by his deceit. *Why is change so slow?*

We're still easily deceived

Every Christian knows that, despite being justified and loved by God as the perfectly obedient Jesus Christ is loved, we remain deeply sinful. Our old sinful nature constantly pleads to be indulged. Let's be honest, we still find sin attractive and we're easily deceived. Take a look at this list of warnings (bold text mine):

Or do you not know that wrongdoers will not inherit the kingdom of God? Do not be **deceived**: Neither the sexually immoral nor idolaters nor adulterers ... will inherit the kingdom of God. (1 Corinthians 6 v 9-10)

But I am afraid that just as Eve was **deceived** by the snake's cunning, your minds may somehow be led astray from your sincere and pure devotion to Christ. (2 Corinthians 11 v 3)

If anyone thinks they are something when they are not, they **deceive** themselves. (Galatians 6 v 3)

Do not be **deceived**: God cannot be mocked. A man reaps what he sows. (Galatians 6 v 7)

But encourage one another daily, as long as it is called "Today", so that none of you may be hardened by sin's **deceitfulness**. (Hebrews 3 v 13)

Do not merely listen to the word, and so **deceive** yourselves. Do what it says. (James 1 v 22)

Those who consider themselves religious and yet do not keep a tight rein on their tongues **deceive** themselves, and their religion is worthless. (James 1 v 26)

We still have the remnant of sin within our earthly natures and so at times we find sin incredibly attractive. We can be mesmerised by it.

There's a great kids' wildlife programme called "Live and Deadly". One Saturday morning I watched with my son as they counted down the "top 30 deadly animals". All the classics were there—sharks, spiders, mosquitoes, hippos. The one I didn't expect came in at number 22: the stoat. *Really?* How are these small furry creatures so deadly? Well, they can kill rabbits more than ten times their size—and they do so by dancing. A stoat will see some rabbits, maybe 200m away, and start some crazy dancing: backflips and contortions. The rabbits are mesmerised and so, rather than run from a deadly enemy, they watch as it gets ever closer. The stoat can dance to a few cm away, before it bites a rabbit at the neck and kills it.

I thought this was extraordinary. The stoat kills a rabbit by dancing it to death!

The Bible warns us that we too can find sin mesmerising. We know it's no good for us but we're captivated, and so rather than running away, we indulge sin until it ensnares us. We can be deceived. That's why we need the word of God to unveil sin's deceit.

Satan's favourite strategies are accusation, temptation and distraction:

1. He *accuses* us of being too sinful for God to accept us—that's why we need the gospel, to know we are wonderfully loved.

2. He *tempts* us by suggesting that sin will make us happier than obeying God's good commands—and again we need the gospel to know that God is for us and wants what is best for us.

3. He *distracts* us with sin so that we don't even realise we're doing anything wrong. Here's where we need the specific rules and commands of Scripture, bluntly reminding us how we're meant to live.

Our minds, though renewed, are still stained by sin. The commands of the New Testament can shake us out of deception and make us realise we need to battle to change.

Do you ever use those funny pink tablets from the dentist? You clean your teeth and think you've done a good job. But when you chew a pink tablet, it reveals a load more plaque that still needs removing. So you have another bout of more vigorous brushing. In some ways, New Testament commands function like this. We may think we're morally okay, but when we take a good dose of Bible commands, we realise there's still sin that desperately needs removing.

So change is slow because we keep being mesmerised by the lies of Satan and captivated by the deceitfulness of sin.

So how do we change?

What advice would you give Peter in his struggle with sin?

Would you tell him to grit his teeth and resist temptation? Or is the best advice, "Believe more deeply what Jesus has done for you and then God will change you"?

I hope by this stage you're clear that in living the Christian life we must allow our *status* before God to shape our *walk* with him. Our status in Jesus Christ is "loved by the Father". Even though we get confused emotionally, these two little statements are always true:

Your STATUS in Christ will shape your walk.

Your walk can never affect your STATUS.

OUR STATUS BEFORE GOD	Our walk with God
UNCHANGING	Fluctuating
COMPLETE	Growing
WE ARE DECLARED HOLY	We are growing in holiness
JUSTIFICATION IS COMPLETE—WE CANNOT INCREASE	Sanctification grows throughout the Christian life and is only perfect in heaven
THE GUILT OF SIN HAS GONE	The corruption of sin is being slowly removed

So, very practically, what advice would you give someone battling to change?

Two oddly competing paths

When we ask how to change in the Christian life, people sometimes bizarrely pit two biblical truths against one another. Let me caricature them crudely:

1. **The "passive" view of change.**
   "Everything in the Christian life is of grace. We're justified by grace alone and we're sanctified (in the sense of moral change) by grace alone. So the only way to change in the Christian life is to believe the gospel more and more. Please don't tell me how to live—just tell me to look at Jesus."

2. **The "active" view:**
   "The New Testament contains loads of commands. I need someone to shout at me to stop mucking about and start pursuing holiness. The best sermons are when the preacher leans close into the microphone and shouts in a voice like Gandalf the wizard, 'Flee temptation you fools!' I love a good beat-up in a sermon."

You can even see the contrast in the different versions of the NIV. In 1984, the editors inserted the title "Rules for Christian living" ahead of Colossians 3 v 1-17. In 2011, this was changed to "Living as those made alive in Christ". That's quite a difference! The old title suggests growth comes from *our work* in obeying rules. The new title implies growth is due to *God's work* in making us alive.

Even within one church you can have people who think the passive route is biblical and complain that the pastor preaches legalistically and lacks grace. Meanwhile others who prefer the active route complain that the pastor hides behind grace and isn't bold enough in telling us to change. I've been accused of both... following the same sermon!

It took me a while to realise that often someone's view is determined by their background. Some people grow up in somewhat legalistic Christian churches and so grow to hate preaching that includes moral exhortation. Others may have led immoral lives, and when they become Christians they are delighted by grace but also love specific moral commands. They delight in the details of obedience.

Are you conscious of which way you lean? The New Testament would tell us that **both** are true. When I get dressed each morning, I put on trousers and a shirt. Please don't tell me to choose between them. It's a false choice that I'm not forced to make (and would look... odd).

Similarly, in spiritual growth we don't choose between a) dwelling upon God's grace or b) fighting hard against sin. We need both. We live out our status as loved children of God by obeying his commands to resist sin. One passage where that's very obvious is Colossians chapter 3.

> [1] Since, then, you have been raised with Christ, set your hearts on things above, where Christ is, seated at the right hand of God. [2] Set your minds on things above, not on earthly things. [3] For you died, and your life is now hidden with Christ in God. [4] When Christ, who is your life, appears, then you also will appear with him in glory.
>
> [5] Put to death, therefore, whatever belongs to your earthly nature: sexual immorality, impurity, lust, evil desires and greed, which is idolatry. [6] Because of these, the wrath of God is coming. (Colossians 3 v 1-6)

Broadly, there are two things we're told to do:

1. Set your thinking on Christ above
2. Put your sin to death

Set your thinking on Christ above

Paul gives us parallel instructions: "Set your hearts" (v 1) and "set your minds" (v 2) on things above, where Christ is. It's not enough to think about heaven, nor is it sufficient to set your emotions there. It needs to be *all* of you.

The key first step in Christian growth is to let your life be shaped by *Christ's* past and future, not your own: "For you died, and your life is now hidden with Christ in God" (v 3).

When you become a Christian, you're united by faith to Jesus. His story becomes yours. No illustration carries this perfectly, but imagine a baby inside a mother's womb. The baby's life is determined by what mum does. If she dives to the bottom of a swimming pool, then so does the baby. If she takes a lift to the top of a skyscraper, so does the baby. If the mother eats hot spicy food, the baby even knows about that! The child is united to its mother, and dependent upon its mother for life, and whatever mum experiences, so does the child.

In a far more profound way, Christ died, has been raised and is seated at the right hand of God. We are united to him and therefore, that's where we're seated too!

Do you notice that in Colossians 3—a chapter that's all about godly living—Paul starts off by fixing our eyes upon Christ? In verses 1-4 we're told to dwell upon him and where he is, because his life and work shapes ours. There's great encouragement here to stop navel-gazing and look at *him*. The key to living the Christian life is *him*. We're raised with Christ, and so the resurrection power of Jesus has broken through into our lives today.

Paul was telling them: "You live in Colossae **and** in Christ". Both are equally true. The world around us shapes us all the time, so to be shaped like Jesus we need to actively set our hearts and minds upon him above. It's not a one-off action like setting a sat nav, which then guides you towards your destination. Here's something we must do repeatedly—set our hearts and minds upon things above.

In other words, our status in Christ is what shapes our walk with him.

Naturally we say, "Yeah, but it's hard. I don't *feel* that I'm united to Christ. I don't *feel* the resurrection power of Jesus within me. I don't seem to be making obvious progress." Maybe, but you are. Set your heart and mind on Christ who is seated above in glory. Allow your life to be shaped by his past and future, and not simply by what you can see of your own life.

These truths do take time to change us.

Who am I?
I'm Matt Fuller. I live in London and my life fluctuates in obedience.
Yet also...
I'm Matt Fuller. I'm hidden with Christ in God and belong with him in glory. *Therefore...*

Put your sin to death

Here's the second thing we're to do. Once we've dwelt upon who we are in Christ and what he has done, then the obligation upon every Christian is to put to death whatever belongs to our earthly nature (v 5). We're to kill sin. *We have fullness in Christ but we still have filthiness within.*

There's a wonderful balance to Paul's teaching here on how to change. It's not purely passive—but nor is it merely fighting in our own strength.

Christians are united to Christ and raised with him. His Spirit dwells within us but we're not merely to "let go and let God". We're to put our sin to death. That's active, violent language. We're not to regret sin—not even to dislike it or hate it. We're to attack it with all our strength. We're to put it to death.

The Puritan John Owen put it in very stark terms:

> *"Be killing sin or sin will be killing you."*

Paul was willing to get very specific about things we should and shouldn't do:

> ⁷ You used to walk in these ways, in the life you once lived. ⁸ But now you must also rid yourselves of all such things as these: anger, rage, malice, slander, and filthy language from your lips. ⁹ Do not lie to each other, since you have taken off your old self with its practices ¹⁰ and have put on the new self, which is being renewed in knowledge in the image of its Creator.
> (Colossians 3 v 7-10)

Having told the Colossians to set their hearts and minds on things above, he can then urge them to change their behaviour. If we think we can ignore the explicit commands of God in our spiritual growth, then we're assuming we know better than the God of the Bible.

If we're going to make progress against the mesmerising power of sin dancing before us, then we need:

1. the gospel to tell us we're loved, and to transform our thinking so that we find obeying Jesus more wonderful than sin.
2. to be commanded to fight with all our strength.

These two always go hand in hand. Set your heart and mind on Christ above *and* actively kill off your sin. Wear trousers *and* a shirt. (Seriously, please do—it's less awkward that way.)

Let's take a simple example. Imagine that someone at work wrongs you. They inflict real loss financially and/or slander your reputation. You try to resolve it with them but they're unwilling and you can't get justice. So you're angry. Really angry. And you want to strike back.

How would Colossians 3 tell you to respond?

1. **Set your hearts and minds on things above.**
   a) Know that you're raised with Christ despite having angered God. He forgave you in Christ.
   b) Embrace the fact that no one was more wronged than Jesus, and yet he could still ask his Father to forgive those who killed him.
   c) Know that you're raised with Christ—the one who rules over ALL things (Colossians 1 v 15-20). He must therefore have good purposes for you in your trial.
   d) Know that one day your life with Christ will be revealed in glory. Even if you never get justice for this wrong, your future is immeasurably wonderful.

2. **Put your sin to death.**
   a) Don't allow your mind to dwell upon what has been done to you.
   b) Don't daydream about humiliating the person who has wronged you.
   c) Don't let your other friends stir you up in anger. Tell them it's best not to talk about it.
   d) If necessary, do something dramatic—move jobs so you have a chance to calm down without seeing this person every day.

It's a bit artificial to work through something in list form like this. It's not as if once we've worked through stage 1 and then stage 2, we're done. We need to keep doing this. We have to keep coming back and drawing down on the resources that Christ gives us in the gospel. It's an inexhaustible bank account of grace that we need to return to time after time.

Yet the basic point is that change comes through the work of God for us and in us, as well as through us taking steps to change.

It's still a work of God!

Please never fall into the trap of thinking that justification is what *God does* for us and sanctification (in the sense of moral change) is what *we do* in our own strength. This a common error that we make. Sanctification is still by the grace of God. It is God's work **in** us and **by** us.

No writer is stronger on the need for Christians to kill sin than John Owen. Yet he also rightly says:

> *"We are commanded to 'wash ourselves', to 'cleanse ourselves from sin', to 'purge ourselves from all our iniquities'... But to suppose that what God requires of us, we have the power ourselves to do is to make the cross and grace of Jesus Christ of no effect ... Whatever God works in us by grace, he prescribes us as duty. He does it in us, yet also he does it by us so that the same work is an act of his Spirit and of our wills." (Complete Works, Vol 3, p 433)*

Years ago I was offered a job as a history teacher at a prestigious London school. I was delighted as I was young at the time, and my previous experience had been at a rough and rowdy school, quite different from the exalted standards expected by the parents and headmaster at this new school.

In the summer before I arrived, my head of department gave me my timetable and told me all the classes I was to teach. He could easily have said, "Well, it's a bit of a coup for you, working at such a prestigious school. Now it's time to pay back our trust by teaching great lessons and securing excellent exam results."

Happily he told me no such thing! He gave me all the books, DVDs and past papers I would need. He sat me down every week to ask if he could help me fill in any gaps in my knowledge or work out the best way to teach a subject. In other words, everything he asked of me, he gave me the resources to complete and was personally involved.

He never asked anything of me without also giving me the resources for the task. He was a good boss, but Jesus is a far better master. He may make great demands of us, but he will always give us the grace and strength to meet them.

How do we change? We set our hearts and minds on where we are because we're united to Jesus. We allow that truth to change us. Then we kill our sin in the strength that God gives us.

So what might you say to Peter as he battles the deceitful attraction of alcohol? I hope it would run something like this:

- Peter, look up and know that Christ has died for your sin and risen to give you new life. Your home is in heaven.
- Know that the power of Christ dwells within you. You're a new creation and can live differently now.
- When the temptation feels overwhelming, look at Christ resisting temptation upon the cross. As he was mocked for not being able to come down and save himself, he resisted that desire in order to save you.

And so:

- Do everything you possibly can to kill your sin. On days when you work from home, give your cash and cards to your wife so you physically can't buy any booze.
- Get a friend to ask you bluntly every fortnight if you've had a drink. Resolve to be honest.
- Have a friend you can call any time of day or night when you think you're about to stumble.
- Do everything you possibly can to fight, and keep setting your heart and mind on Christ in heaven so that you have the desire to keep fighting.

Then, what about you?

Are you aware of what sins you're most mesmerised by? Let the word of God expose your flaws; then take time to set your heart and mind on Christ above... and fight!

9. Why are believers warned not to fall away?

No one enjoys warnings.

Some of them seem a bit silly. My new iron came with the warning, "Do not iron clothes while wearing them". Thanks, but I'm not an idiot.

Others we take mild offence at. We find it patronising when someone says, "Don't forget your passport," because it suggests we're forgetful.

Still other warnings we dislike because, well, they're a bit upsetting. The sign on the beach that says, "Don't swim in the sea—dangerous jellyfish" is useful. It might even save our life. The road sign that says, "Eight people died in road accidents on this road last year" is distressing, but it might prevent another accident.

So while they may be be upsetting, we do accept sensible warnings. They have their place and are necessary.

The same is true in the Christian life. We may not like warnings but they're one means the Lord uses to keep us going.

Given all we've said in this book, it's natural to ask, "If God has promised that we can never lose our justification and that he will never let us go, why does he warn us not to fall away?" How do these warnings fit with our unconditional status?

Or, to rephrase the question, how do promises like these...

> My sheep listen to my voice; I know them, and they follow me. I give them eternal life, and they shall never perish; no one will snatch them out of my hand. My Father, who has given them to me, is greater than all; no one can snatch them out of my Father's hand.
> (John 10 v 27-29)

> For I am convinced that neither death nor life, neither angels nor demons, neither the present nor the future, nor any powers, neither height nor depth, nor anything else in all creation, will be able to separate us from the love of God that is in Christ Jesus our Lord.
> (Romans 8 v 38-39)

... co-exist with warnings like these:

> If you do not remain in me, you are like a branch that is thrown away and withers; such branches are picked up, thrown into the fire and burned. (John 15 v 6)

> The Spirit clearly says that in later times some will abandon the faith and follow deceiving spirits and things taught by demons. (1 Timothy 4 v 1)

Before we look carefully at the answer, let me say up front that the warnings given in Scripture do not cancel out or *in any way* weaken God's promises that his love is unchanging and that he will never let a believer go.

A parent might promise to her six-year-old, "I will always keep you safe". She might also warn, "If you play with matches, you'll get burned". The warning doesn't weaken the promise.

Rather, it helps the mother keep the promise.

Of course, the promises of a parent are fallible: they cannot guarantee safety. That's different with God's promises. They cannot fail. Yet one way God maintains his promise to keep us is by using warnings.

OUR STATUS BEFORE GOD	Our walk with God
UNCONDITIONAL	Conditional
UNCHANGING	Fluctuating
HE WILL NEVER LET US GO	We are warned never to leave

The church is a mixed-up place

Warnings only work on those who are genuinely Christians—and the New Testament is clear that *not everyone who belongs to a church is a genuine Christian*. Jesus and his apostles are clear that most churches have a mixture of people. Some will have genuine faith; and some will not. We saw in chapter five that the New Testament speaks of a group of people with *spurious* faith—and that, by contrast, *genuine* faith always transforms people so that they grow in holiness. One further mark of genuine faith is that it perseveres. Not everyone who professes faith in Jesus does that:

> The seed falling on rocky ground refers to someone who hears the word and at once receives it with joy. But since they have no root, they last only a short time. When trouble or persecution comes because of the word, they quickly fall away. (Matthew 13 v 20-21)

> But now [God] has reconciled you by Christ's physical body through death to present you holy in his sight, without blemish and free from accusation—if you continue in your faith, established and firm, and do not

move from the hope held out in the gospel. (Colossians
1 v 22-23)

They went out from us, but they did not really belong
to us. For if they had belonged to us, they would have
remained with us; but their going showed that none of
them belonged to us. (1 John 2 v 19)

In Matthew 13, Jesus describes a person who hears the
gospel with great joy but then falls away. They were never
truly believers. Paul tells the Colossians that the true believer
knows that they're reconciled to God IF they continue in the
faith. John tells his audience that some former members of
the church left, showing they were never truly Christians.

So the warnings of the New Testament are not merely
hypothetical. Some people currently sitting in churches will,
in time, turn away from Christ—showing they were never
truly born again.

By contrast, genuine faith keeps going. Those whom God
has justified he *will* glorify (Romans 8 v 30).

We need encouragement
All of us, though, need encouragement to keep going as
Christians. Some of the strongest warnings in the New
Testament come in the book of Hebrews, and we'll spend most
of this chapter there. Yet throughout that book, the warnings
dance in tandem with God's wonderful promises. The
writer describes what he's written as a "word of exhortation"
(Hebrews 13 v 22). This word "exhortation" is often translated
as "encouragement". Both convey the meaning well.

Sometimes we need affirming encouragement. You might
imagine a parent telling a child before an exam, "You'll do fine.
You've worked hard, you know the stuff and your previous results

have been great." At other times we need stirring encouragement. You might imagine a parent, passionately screaming on the sides of the football field, "Don't give up. Get up and have another go! The game's not over yet! Keep running!"

Hebrews has both affirming and stirring encouragement. The warnings are part of the stirring-up exhortation.

Trampling upon Jesus

We must be clear on what precisely the writer is warning against. The sermon to the Hebrews is addressed to readers who are in real danger of apostasy—the complete and calculated rejection of Christ. The writer's audience was in danger of ignoring the word of God and turning away from Christ as their high priest. Look at the strength of these warnings:

> We must pay the most careful attention, therefore, to what we have heard, so that we do not drift away. For since the message spoken through angels was binding, and every violation and disobedience received its just punishment, how shall we escape if we ignore so great a salvation? (Hebrews 2 v 1-3)

> See to it, brothers and sisters, that none of you has a sinful, unbelieving heart that turns away from the living God ... We have come to share in Christ, if indeed we hold our original conviction firmly to the very end. (Hebrews 3 v 12, 14)

> [26] If we deliberately keep on sinning after we have received the knowledge of the truth, no sacrifice for sins is left, [27] but only a fearful expectation of judgment and of raging fire that will consume the enemies of God. [28] Anyone who rejected the law of Moses died without mercy on the testimony of two or three witnesses.

> [29] How much more severely do you think someone deserves to be punished who has trampled the Son of God underfoot, who has treated as an unholy thing the blood of the covenant that sanctified them, and who has insulted the Spirit of grace? (Hebrews 10 v 26-29)

> Make every effort to live in peace with everyone and to be holy; without holiness no one will see the Lord. See to it that no one falls short of the grace of God.
> (Hebrews 12 v 14-15)

These all refer to the same problem. The sin the author is concerned about is a deliberate and irreversible rejection of Jesus. He is **not** warning that if you stumble into sin for a while, before repenting, you'll be cut off. He is **not** warning that if you're wrong on one minor area of doctrine, you're cut off. He **is** warning that if you consciously and publicly turn away from Christ and insult the Spirit (Hebrews 6 v 6; 10 v 29), then there's no salvation for you, only judgment.

So, can I say very loudly, that if you're worried that these warnings apply to you, it's unlikely they do. The writer is describing people who once trusted Christ but are now showing disdain for him and have renounced the faith. People like that don't worry about committing apostasy; they're pleased to have done so!

Let's focus on one passage in Hebrews (5 v 11 – 6 v 12) to see how the warnings work alongside the positive encouragements of the writer.

Don't be sluggish hearers

Recently, as part of a game, I was asked to describe my wife in five words. It's a bizarre exercise (try it of anyone you love). A word I certainly didn't use was "sluggish". No one wants to be called that. Yet (although it's translated as "lazy" or "no longer trying" in the NIV) that's literally what the author calls the Hebrews. The section is framed by twin references to being sluggish. Let me translate them this way:

> We have much to say about this, but it is hard to make it clear to you because you have become **sluggish** of hearing. (Hebrews 5 v 11)

> We do not want you to become **sluggish**, but to imitate those who through faith and patience inherit what has been promised. (Hebrews 6 v 12)

He warns them that how they respond to the word of God *today* is an indicator that they're born again and will persevere. He expects believers to be moving forward in the Christian life—not to be slugs who are drifting away!

> Therefore let us move beyond the elementary teachings about Christ and be taken forward to maturity, not laying again the foundation of repentance from acts that lead to death, and of faith in God, instruction about cleansing rites, the laying on of hands, the resurrection of the dead, and eternal judgment. And God permitting, we will do so. (Hebrews 6 v 1-3)

Here again the writer expects Christians to be moving forward in their faith. It's unlikely that happens *every* day and probably not *every* week. Yet, although there are dips and stumbles, the overall direction is forward.

The foundation of the Christian life is repentance and faith. You never move on from that, but you do want to build on it. The foundations of a skyscraper are crucial. You don't want to lay them again, but it would be weird to dig foundations but never construct the other floors.

It's impossible for Christ-haters to be brought back

There's a shift at verse 4. Instead of addressing everyone and saying "let us" (as he did in verse 1), the writer turns to give a stark warning:

> 4 It is impossible for those who have once been enlightened, who have tasted the heavenly gift, who have shared in the Holy Spirit, 5 who have tasted the goodness of the word of God and the powers of the coming age 6 and who have fallen away, to be brought back to repentance. To their loss they are crucifying the Son of God all over again and subjecting him to public disgrace. (Hebrews 6 v 4-6)

Let's again ask:

Q: Can a Christian "fall away" and lose their salvation?
A: No. But some who make a profession of faith were never genuinely converted.

Verses 4-5 are NOT describing a Christian. They're describing someone who has spent time in church, assumed they're a believer and yet never were. The phrases used of such a person are strong, but the writer seems to be taking language from the book of Exodus. Back then, plenty of Israelites...

- were "enlightened"—they were led by a pillar of fire through the wilderness.
- "tasted the heavenly gift"—they tasted manna falling from heaven.
- "shared in the Spirit's work"—the Spirit of God dwelt among them in the tabernacle.
- "tasted the goodness of God's word"—Moses preached it to them.

- "tasted the powers of the coming age"—they saw signs and wonders such as the parting of the Red Sea.

Yet many of them never entered the promised land. They simply did not have saving faith (Hebrews 4 v 2).

The picture of verses 7-8 clarifies that the person who has fallen away in verse 6 was never truly a believer:

> Land that drinks in the rain often falling on it and that produces a crop useful to those for whom it is farmed receives the blessing of God. But land that produces thorns and thistles is worthless and is in danger of being cursed. In the end it will be burned. (Hebrews 6 v 7-8)

The picture isn't of land that was once useful but then becomes worthless. Rather, it's a picture of the same rain falling on two types of soil. The first land produces useful crops; the second land worthless crops. It's a similar picture to the parable of the soils that Jesus tells in Matthew 13 v 1-23. Some land may initially appear to be producing fruit, but time reveals that it's not.

Q. Why is it impossible for people like this to be brought back to repentance?

A. Nothing is impossible for God, but the writer is describing people who don't want to be brought back. They take pleasure in publicly mocking Jesus.

The writer paints a bleak picture by way of warning. He's saying: "DON'T DO THAT!" It's similar to anti-smoking warnings. In some parts of the world, every cigarette pack has a gruesome picture of blackened lungs or a deformed tongue due to tobacco use. They're grim pictures and somewhat shocking. They make the point that some who continue to smoke will end up like this. Don't be one of them. Take action today.

Hebrews is saying, *Don't be sluggish hearers who drift into abandoning Jesus. Respond to God's word today!*

Believers will inherit what is promised

Having issued his warning, the writer changes tone in verse 9. Look at how he addresses the readers.

> 9 Even though we speak like this, dear friends, we are convinced of better things in your case—the things that have to do with salvation. 10 God is not unjust; he will not forget your work and the love you have shown him as you have helped his people and continue to help them. 11 We want each of you to show this same diligence to the very end, so that what you hope for may be fully realised. 12 We do not want you to become lazy, but to imitate those who through faith and patience inherit what has been promised. (Hebrews 6 v 9-12)

He is "convinced" that they'll respond and so avoid the fate of those who have turned away. He calls them "dear friends"—the only time he uses that term in the book. He also returns to using "you". So the section runs:

- 5 v 11 – 6 v 3   YOU have a problem
- 6 v 4-8   Those who subject Jesus to public disgrace can't be brought back
- 6 v 9-12   but YOU have a better future than that

Q. How do I know which I am? Am I someone who will in the future fall away OR am I a dear friend?
A. Don't fall away!

The writer is clear that the Lord will never let a believer go. Yet he doesn't answer the question for any individual.

He doesn't say, "It's impossible for you, Matt, to fall away".
Nor does he say, "Matt, I think you might fall away".
He simply says, "Don't fall away!"

Why is the writer so confident in verses 9-12? There are two big reasons: 1) their love for others (v 10-11) and 2) God's promises (v 12). Which means that when we're a little shaken by hearing a warning from God, we should do two things:

1. Continue to diligently serve other people. Putting ourselves out for others at church is a mark of God's Spirit in us. Making costly sacrifices of time and money for others helps to bring assurance that our faith is real. It tends to be lazy Christians who aren't involved in church who begin to doubt their salvation. Joyful obedience tends to wash away doubts.

2. Keep trusting God's promises (v 12). The writer is realistic—it takes faith in Jesus *and patience* to inherit eternal life. But what promises we have to cling to! As he goes on to say in the rest of chapter six, the Lord is a God who cannot lie. Jesus has gone ahead of us to heaven, and because we're united to him we will *join* him one day:

> We have this hope as an anchor for the soul, firm and secure. It enters the inner sanctuary behind the curtain, where our forerunner, Jesus, has entered on our behalf. He has become a high priest for ever.
> (Hebrews 6 v 19-20)

It's such a beautiful phrase. Our hope in Jesus is *an anchor for the soul*. He is the place we look to for certainty that we'll make it to glory.

How do we hear God's warnings?

I can't really tell you how to hear a warning of God. At this moment of your life you may need the warning, "Don't be sluggish in your faith. You're walking a path which ends in rejecting Jesus." Then again, it could be you need to hear, "You're going well. Just keep going."

But let me say again that God's warnings do not weaken his promises to never let us go and to always love us. A colleague at church puts it this way: Imagine the life of salvation as a long road that believers drive down. God has promised he will get us to the end of this road and that we'll arrive at heaven. How might he keep his promise?

One option would be to erect massive barriers to prevent us going off the road. (I'm imagining the bumpers they put up at a bowling alley when there's a kids' party.) We may career from one side of the road to the other. We may have a miserable time hitting the barriers repeatedly. But we'll eventually make it.

The other (biblical) option is that every couple of miles along the road, God erects massive signs saying, "Danger. Stay on the road." He regularly takes over the car radio to give encouraging messages: "I will make sure you get home". Best of all, God puts a driving instructor in the passenger seat who tells us to take the warnings seriously. At desperate times, he grabs the wheel and keeps us going straight.

It's not a perfect example, but God chooses to keep his promise to us in a manner similar to the second road description. He has erected warnings in Scripture alongside his promises to us. Yet he's also given us his Spirit to keep us going. The Spirit ensures that when we're in danger of sliding off the road, we hear a warning clearly and get ourselves straight again.

So, the book of Hebrews, with its frequent warnings, still ends with emphasis upon the promises and work of God:

> God has said, "Never will I leave you; never will I forsake you." (Hebrews 13 v 5)

> Now may the God of peace, who through the blood of the eternal covenant brought back from the dead our Lord Jesus, that great Shepherd of the sheep, equip you with everything good for doing his will, and may he work in us what is pleasing to him. (Hebrews 13 v 20-21)

10. How do I enjoy greater assurance of God's love?

When I die, I'm going to be with Jesus in paradise. I'm 100% certain of that fact.

If you're a Christian, then I hope you are too.

It's not an arrogant statement; it's plain biblical thought. My confidence is not based upon myself, but upon Jesus.

That confidence or assurance was one of the defining marks that distinguished the Reformers from the medieval Roman Catholic church. It's still a dividing line between biblical faith and distortions today.

The Christian can say, "No doubts, no uncertainty. I'm going to live with God for ever, despite my behaviour. I'm going to paradise because I'm united to Jesus."

Yet one of the lingering effects of sin is that most of us struggle with assurance at some point.

By assurance I mean the inward sense of peace that I'm in right standing with God now due to my union with Christ, and that he will take me to be with him for ever.

The Lord wants us to have that joy and peace:

> I write these things to you who believe in the name of
> the Son of God so that you may know that you have
> eternal life. (1 John 5 v 13)

John is saying it's quite possible to believe in the Son of God, yet *doubt* that you have eternal life. It's quite possible to have faith but not enjoy assurance. When we know we've sinned, when we know there are inconsistencies in our life, there are times when, even though we have faith, we still wonder if we're loved.

And sometimes people lack assurance for good reason. They're stuck in a pattern of deliberate, unrepentant sin. As we saw in the last chapter, sometimes people need warning.

Imagine that three people came to you and each said, "I'm not sure I'm a Christian". What would you say? Let's caricature them:

- Person A was enduring a tough time in life and so wondered if God had abandoned them.
- Person B was a hard-hearted hypocrite who visited prostitutes several times a week and rarely turned up to church.
- Person C was a young woman with a tender conscience who was conscious of daily sins but confessed them regularly and was growing in her faith.

I hope our answers would be different to these three!

Let's briefly think about three responses:

1. Trust the Father's discipline
2. Observe the Spirit
3. Above all, look to Christ

1. Trust the Father's discipline

One question we've not yet touched on is that of the Lord's discipline of Christians. We sometimes get a little confused:

Q: If Jesus has taken all my punishment for sin, why does the Bible still speak of God's discipline and chastening of believers?

A: The Lord's discipline of believers is **not** the penalty imposed by a judge but the loving training of a father.

Our loving Father allows, and indeed plans, for us to be disciplined so that we grow in holiness.

It's so important we know this, so that we don't judge the Lord's love for us by our circumstances!

> 4 In your struggle against sin, you have not yet resisted to the point of shedding your blood. 5 And have you completely forgotten this word of encouragement that addresses you as a father addresses his son? It says,
>
> > "My son, do not make light of the Lord's discipline,
> >   and do not lose heart when he rebukes you,
> > 6 because the Lord disciplines the one he loves,
> >   and he chastens everyone he accepts as his son."
>
> 7 Endure hardship as discipline; God is treating you as his children. For what children are not disciplined by their father? 8 If you are not disciplined—and everyone undergoes discipline —then you are not legitimate, not true sons and daughters at all. 9 Moreover, we have all had human fathers who disciplined us and we respected them for it. How much more should we submit to the Father of spirits and live! 10 They disciplined us for a little while as they thought best; but God disciplines us for our good, in order that we may share in his

holiness. ¹¹ No discipline seems pleasant at the time, but painful. Later on, however, it produces a harvest of righteousness and peace for those who have been trained by it. (Hebrews 12 v 4-11)

Discipline tends to be for one of two reasons:

- It can be for **neutral reasons**. Imagine a man who wants to run a marathon. Every week he meets with a personal trainer to be disciplined in exercise. It really hurts! Sometimes he's stretched to the point of exhaustion. He's not done anything wrong, but he needs the discipline to become stronger.

- It can also be for **naughty reasons**. After a child has pinched her little brother, her parents discipline her and she's upset. Here the girl has done something wrong and needs disciplining to learn how to behave.

The Lord disciplines us for *both* of these reasons, and we're often unable to discern which it is. When it feels as if we're being disciplined, we may not know if it's a response to a specific "naughty" sin or more neutral discipline to help us grow into maturity. That's okay. We don't need to know. We should confess anything we're conscious we've done wrong, and keep trusting the Lord.

He places us in painful circumstances so that we may learn to become more like him. It's so important to know this, so that we don't doubt the Father's love when life is tough.

Hebrews 12 tells us that, "The Lord disciplines the one he loves" (v 6). Indeed, discipline is a mark of being a true son or daughter (v 8). His discipline is for our good. God's purpose is to produce "a harvest of righteousness and peace" (v 11). His discipline trains us to become more like him in holiness (v 10) with the benefits *now* of righteous living and peace in our conscience. His discipline is a mark of his love and determination to train us so that we keep going all the way to the new creation. Then we'll fully share his holiness.

So, if in times of hardship we say, "I hate God's discipline", we're not asking for *more* love from God but *less*. He loves us so much that he'll use painful events to help us to grow in holiness and become more like him.

So, please don't doubt God's love for you when life is painful. Don't think that when you sin there's anything you need to pay off to "top up" Christ's work. The Puritan writer Samuel Bolton expressed it beautifully:

> *"Christ for us having endured all the wrath of the Father, his love only remains to us. The dark and deadly shower fell with all its heaviest drops upon his devoted head, while upon us descends a sunshine dew with kindly warmth and moisture to soften the hard soil of our hearts and cause them to bring forth fruits of holiness.*
>
> *Christ drank to the dregs that bitter cup which would have consigned us to eternal condemnation, and left for us a salutary medicine—chastisement instead of punishment, correction instead of a sentence."*

It's when we look to Christ and are reminded of what he has done that we can begin to feel and know the Father's discipline as a "sunshine dew" and not a "dark shower".

2. Observe the Spirit

There are numerous places in the New Testament where we're told to look at the Spirit's work in transforming us in order to be assured of our faith:

> We know that we have come to know him if we keep his
> commands. Whoever says, "I know him," but does not
> do what he commands is a liar, and the truth is not in
> that person. (1 John 2 v 3-4)

> Let us not love with words or speech but with actions
> and in truth. This is how we know that we belong to the
> truth and how we set our hearts at rest in his presence.
> (1 John 3 v 18-19)

John is saying that Christians should be able to look to see how they've changed since coming to faith. For those who've been believers for many years, there should be some progress. Sometimes we struggle to see it in ourselves, much as a child is often not aware of growing taller. We need to encourage one another that there has been growth. As we've said before, what God declares *of us* in justification, he works out *in us* by gradual transformation.

Throughout his letters, John uses black-and-white language to suggest that Christians do not sin. Yet by this he does not mean *perfection*, but determined *progress*. There's a difference between falling in a lake by accident and deliberately jumping in every day. This side of heaven, all Christians continue to sin. We don't desire to fall in, but we do. That's very different from wilfully planning to jump into sin repeatedly, and never doing anything to address the habit.

If you've made progress in obeying the Lord and loving others, then give thanks for those marks of the Spirit at work within you. Yet do remember, as we said in chapter five, that growing godliness *confirms* justification by faith alone. Our godliness and good works can never *replace* it.

You can normally tell when this is beginning to happen: we become proud and self-righteous! The proud person says, "My holiness has grown. Well done, me!" But the healthy believer recognises that they've grown and gives thanks to God for his grace in that change.

3. Above all, look to Christ

This is always the most important action to take when lacking assurance! Can I remind you of what we said in chapter two? Stop looking at yourself and your behaviour, and look at him.

It was back in 1863 that Charitie Lees Bancroft first published a hymn she called "The Advocate". I'm told it was originally written as a children's hymn—but it's one we never move on from, and now sing often as "Before the throne of God above".

Nervous Christians need to sing loudly.

When Satan tempts me to despair
And tells me of the guilt within,
Upward I look and see him there
Who made an end of all my sin.
Because the sinless Saviour died,
My sinful soul is counted free,
For God the just is satisfied
To look on him and pardon me.

The whole song is a beautiful summary of the book of Hebrews, with its great emphasis upon the confidence we have in the finished work of Jesus for us:

Therefore, brothers and sisters, since we have
confidence to enter the Most Holy Place by the blood
of Jesus, by a new and living way opened for us through
the curtain, that is, his body, and since we have a great
priest over the house of God, let us draw near to God
with a sincere heart and with the full assurance that faith

brings, having our hearts sprinkled to cleanse us from a guilty conscience and having our bodies washed with pure water. (Hebrews 10 v 19-22)

Keep looking to him.

In the end, assurance—the inward sense of peace—is hard to find unless we spend time with the Lord. I'll say again, you can have a saving faith without assurance. But why choose that? It's certainly not the Father's desire for his children. Let me finish with one lengthy quote from the 19th-century preacher J. C. Ryle, from a sermon on John 3 v 16:

> *"Would you have more faith? Do you find believing so pleasant that you would like to believe more? Then take heed that you are diligent in the use of every means of grace—diligent in your private communion with God— diligent in your daily watchfulness over time, temper, and tongue—diligent in your private Bible reading—diligent in your own private prayers. It is vain to expect spiritual prosperity, when we are careless about these things. Let those who will, call it over-precise and legal to be particular about them. I only reply, that there never was an eminent saint who neglected them.*
>
> *Would you have more faith? Then seek to become more acquainted with Jesus Christ. Study your blessed Saviour more and more, and strive to know more of the length and breadth and height of his love. Study him in all his offices— as the Priest, the Physician, the Redeemer, the Advocate, the Friend, the Teacher, the Shepherd of his believing people. Study him as one who not only died for you—but is also living for you at the right hand of God—as one who not only shed his blood for you—but daily intercedes for you at the right hand of God—as one who is soon coming*

again for you, and will stand once more on this earth. The
miner who is fully persuaded that the rope which draws him
up from the pit will not break, is drawn up without anxiety
and alarm. The believer who is thoroughly acquainted with
the fullness of Jesus Christ—is the believer who travels from
grace to glory with the greatest comfort and peace. Then
let your daily prayers always contain these words, 'Lord,
increase my faith'."

In other words, *stop looking at yourself and look at him*. Looking
at him takes an investment of time in Bible reading and
prayer. But diligently listening to him and praying to him is
the way to know the deepest joy and greatest assurance in the
Christian life. Look away from yourself and look at him.

So, to return to our three friends from the beginning of
the chapter who were wondering if they were truly Christians:

- Person A, enduring a tough time in life, wondered
  if God had abandoned them. They need to be
  encouraged that God is a good Father who grants
  the discipline we need for our good.
- Person B was a hard-hearted hypocrite visiting
  prostitutes and avoiding church. He needs to be
  warned that he can have no confidence that he's saved.
  The person that God justifies he also transforms by
  his Spirit. So this hypocrite needs to repent!
- Person C was the young woman with a tender
  conscience. She needs to look to Christ and return
  to the throne of God above!

It's faith that saves us, not assurance. But having full assurance
in God's work is the best way to work out our salvation! It's
what the Lord desires for us.

A final word: Perfection is eternal; sin is not

We currently live our lives as "perfect" and as "sinners".
We are perfectly justified and loved by God as our Father. That will never end.

But sin will end.

In the new creation we will be "simply" perfect. When Christ returns, our justification will be declared before all creation and we'll be perfected.

The Bible happily gives us a variety of pictures of our future in glory and yet, the things we are shown about the new creation are only seen in comparison with this sinful earth. It's surely going to be far greater than all we can ask or imagine!

There will be no more sin in us

I'm not sure I dwell upon this wonderful truth enough. Here are some of the things we know will be true:

We'll not battle against sin

> Nothing impure will ever enter it ... but only those whose names are written in the Lamb's book of life.
>
> (Revelation 21 v 27)

There is no sin in heaven and there can be no sin in us. We'll all be given a white robe (Revelation 6 v 11) to show we're without sin. Won't that be wonderful?!

No longer will we know the temptation to do wrong. No longer the frustration of falling into sin. No longer the misery of causing hurt. No longer times of losing in our battle. We will sin no more.

We'll cherish Christ rightly

> Dear friends, now we are children of God, and what we will be has not yet been made known. But we know that when Christ appears, we shall be like him, for we shall see him as he is. (1 John 3 v 2)

How wonderful that I'll never again have a devotional time that's dry and leaves me unaffected. We will see Christ, hear his voice and respond passionately. It will be impossible to "go through the motions" of the Christian faith. Impossible to be half-hearted. Impossible to doubt.

We'll delight in others truly

It's frustrating that here on earth, there are Christians we don't always see eye to eye with. They're our brothers and sisters, yet we disagree on some issues and ideas. We're a little nervous in their company; we're careful with what we say in case we cause offence or irritate them. I'm so looking forward to being perfectly one in heart and mind.

We'll also fully enjoy the gifts others have without any hint of jealousy. The green-eyed monster is locked out of heaven.

Will we remember our sins?

I'm not sure the Bible addresses this question directly, yet it's one I've been asked plenty of times. How can we rejoice in being forgiven but not look back in pain at our sin? In the end, we trust the Lord with this question, yet I think we are pointed towards the answer.

There are many wonderful descriptions of how the Lord views our sin. It is blotted out, wiped out, not remembered and cast into the depths of the sea (Isaiah 43 v 25; Acts 3 v 19; Hebrews 8 v 12; Micah 7 v 19). But these are descriptions of the guilt and consequences of our sin. It's not that the Lord has selective amnesia. He *chooses* to not remember sin. The point is that our sin and its consequences cannot be found because they have been dealt with.

We know that, even now, the degree of our love for Christ is connected with the awareness of how deep our debt of sin is. As Jesus explained to Simon the Pharisee:

> You did not put oil on my head, but she has poured
> perfume on my feet. Therefore, I tell you, her many sins
> have been forgiven—as her great love has shown. But
> whoever has been forgiven little loves little.
> (Luke 7 v 46-47)

It seems that in heaven right now, the song of the Lamb is founded upon a recollection of sin:

> And they sang a new song, saying:
> "You are worthy to take the scroll and to open its
> seals, because you were slain, and with your blood
> you purchased for God persons from every tribe and

language and people and nation. You have made them
to be a kingdom and priests to serve our God, and they
will reign on the earth." (Revelation 5 v 9-10)

The blood of Jesus purchases us out of our slavery to sin. That's what he's being praised for.

So I think we will have an awareness of our sin, but that in our sinless state, it will not cause us distress.

We'll know the sweetness of being forgiven but not the shame for what we've done.

In the meantime, we live as children of God. We're justified, loved and secure, united to Jesus Christ. We seek to put sin to death, even as we trust God's promises that we are perfect before him.

Sin will end; perfection will not. What a day that will be.

Oh, that day when freed from sinning,
I shall see thy lovely face;
Clothed then in the blood-washed linen
How I'll sing thy wondrous grace!
Come, my Lord, no longer tarry,
Take my ransomed soul away;
Send thine angels soon to carry
Me to realms of endless day.
(Robert Robinson, 1758)

For further reading

Each chapter of this little book covers a considerable area of Christian doctrine. I've noted the books I've referenced. These would be helpful for further reading in each area.

Chapter One

- I enjoyed James Buchanan's classic *The Doctrine of Justification* (Banner of Truth reprint 1984), especially chapter 10 on justice.

Chapter Two

- To my mind, the best recent primer on justification for pastors to read is *Faith Alone* by Tom Schreiner (Zondervan 2015).
- A great book on seeing justification in its correct place is *One with Christ* by Marcus Johnson (Crossway 2013).

Chapter Three

- The references to John Owen come from *Communion with the Triune God* (Crossway 2007, p 117).
- The illustration from Garry Williams is from *His love endures forever* (IVP 2015, p 169).
- The chapter on adoption in *Knowing God* by James Packer is worth reading once a year! (Hodder, reprint 1993)

Chapter Four

- A helpful book to explore this in great depth is *Antinomianism* by Mark Jones (P&R 2013).

Chapter Five

- Charles Spurgeon: *Faith—what is it? How can it be obtained?* (Sermon #1609, Metropolitan Tabernacle).

Chapter Six

- The quote from Christopher Ash comes from *Pure Joy* (IVP 2012, p 92). The whole book is excellent on the role the conscience plays in Christian living.

Chapter Seven

- The quotes of Jonathan Edwards come from his sermon *The Portion of the Righteous*.
- The quotes from C. S. Lewis come from his sermon: *C. S. Lewis, The Weight of Glory*.

- If you want a dissenting voice that denies that there are variable rewards in heaven I found Craig Blomberg's essay *Degrees of reward in heaven?* very stimulating, if not in the end persuasive.

All these were accessed online.

Chapter Eight

- John Owen: *The Holy Spirit, Complete Works Vol 3.* (Banner of Truth, reprint 2013). The quotes come from p 124.

Chapter Nine

- Wayne Grudem's chapter on the "Warnings in Hebrews" in *Still Sovereign*, edited by Tom Schreiner (Baker 2001).
- Peter O'Brien: *God has spoken in his Son: A biblical theology of Hebrews* (Apollos 2016). He is particularly persuasive on the Exodus backdrop for the references in chapter 6.

Chapter Ten

- Samuel Bolton: *The True Bounds of Christian Freedom*, p 96 (Banner reprint 2001). I'm grateful to my colleague Phil Allcock for sharing this quote and his pastoral wisdom in the area of God's discipline.
- The J. C. Ryle quote comes from a sermon on John 3 v 16 titled *Faith*. Freely available online.

A final word

- I found John Newton's Letter III to Rev. Dr. Hawies persuasive on "Will we remember sin?"

Thank you...

I'm grateful to those who encouraged me to write this, especially Stephen, Katie and Harriet; you really spurred me on. Thanks to Garry, Christopher, Andy, Phil and Ceri for improving the original draft. And many thanks to Alison for patient work in editing, especially during a painful season.